VOLUME 29   NUMBER 1   2023

The Science of Sex Itself

Edited by Benjamin Kahan and Greta LaFleur

HOW TO DO THE HISTORY OF SEXUAL SCIENCE

Benjamin Kahan and Greta LaFleur

There is always more surface to a shattered object than a whole
object, and likewise the surfaces of a fragment are less "cheering."
—Djuna Barnes, letter to Emily Holmes Coleman, 1935

$\mathcal{S}$exology is a shattered object that was never whole. Its broken fragments, dif-
fused across the globe, have lacerated sexual life into some decidedly uncheerful
shapes, lending violent structure while nonetheless creating new possibilities and
new forms. This special issue gauges how sexual science's pasts and shattered
but newly instantiated presents inform constructions of sex, sexuality, and gender,
understanding sexology as both something that we're returning to with increased
interest and something we're living in.[1] It will trace not just sexual science's travels
but also its modes and methods of transport, its movement across paths, sometimes
difficult to follow and retrace. The title of this special issue—"The Science of Sex
Itself"—encapsulates this difficulty, animating the oddly placed emphatic and
reflexive pronoun "itself" to gesture to how the study of sexology, even while ineluctably entwined with the study of sexuality, has its own motor force, laying claim to
objects, regions, questions, and authority distinct from those that have historically
been at the heart of sexuality studies. Before, between, and alongside Gayle Rubin's
(2012: 137–81) theorizing of sexual practice as a vector of oppression, or Roderick Ferguson's (2004) anatomization of Black sociosexual cultures as the target of
increased state and private regulation, some of the core concepts of early sexual
science—deviance, sexual maturity, a normative sense of sexual functionality—
had provided a hegemonic grounding for the elaboration of racialized sexual mores
surrounding gender and sexual comportment. At the same time, sex *itself*, with its

GLQ 29:1
DOI 10.1215/10642684-10144350
© 2023 by Duke University Press

doubling insistence that seems to insist *too much*, calls into question our sense of surety about sexual science as a chronologically delimited object that spans the middle of the nineteenth and twentieth centuries.[2] That is, the unmoored and unmooring *itself* threatens to fracture and disperse the object's solidity, asking: what *is* sexology? What are the limits or the extent of the sexological?

Pinning down what, exactly, sexology *is*, and how we might recognize traces of, as Joan Lubin and Jeanne Vaccaro (2021: 6) put it, "the undead qualit[ies] of sexual science" in our current moment is profoundly difficult. While there is certainly some strategic use to invoking, as many have before us, Janice Irvine's (2005: 1–2) characterization of sexology as "an umbrella term denoting the activity of a multidisciplinary group of researchers, clinicians, and educators concerned with sexuality," there is still much scholarship, writing, and even state discipline that concerns itself with sex but that is still, nonetheless, not *sexology* or *sexological*.[3] Thus, one of the first tasks as we conceptualized this special issue was to figure out what we mean when we name sexology as one of the intellectual genealogies of a formation—sexual difference, for example, or the racialization of gender—and how to distinguish between what might be termed a sexological account of sex, sexual difference, or sexuality, and a less sexological or nonsexological account thereof.

If not all understandings of gender and sexuality are significantly inflected by sexology, and not all legacies of the sexological have anything to do with sex or sexuality, then how do we effectively think with what we have called, between ourselves, the "squishiness" of sexology as a highly porous and widely influential field of the human sciences—and a field that also may not *really* be part of the human sciences at all?[4] If the porousness of this putative field—its capacity to soak up and incorporate parts of other disciplines, practices, and fields of knowledge—renders sexology somewhat shapeless, able to expand and contract, how do we narrate its histories and chart its lines of force? How do we make sense of the use of sexology as a discipline dedicated to the study of gender and sexuality, even as some of the most well-documented uses of sexological literatures have not been the *study* of sexuality so much as the *practice* of it, for this genre of print has historically provided some of the most tried-and-true outlets for the more masturbatory inclinations of a certain echelon of the population—learned treatise or spank bank? Indeed, if the limits of the sexological are blurred by its more innocuous disreputability—it has never shaken the taint of the pseudoscientific, the paraprofessional (Wolffram 2009)—its proximity, too, to the occult (Dixon 1997), obscenity, pornography (Cocks 2004; Bull 2021), and quackery amplifies the uncertainty that envelops its epistemological nature and authoritative value.

To say that the contents or limits of what might fall within the purview of the sexological are uncertain and can never be clearly delineated, however, is not to abjure the pressures it has exerted on the material world. Indeed, it is precisely sexual science's protean portability that has enabled it to worm its way into so many matrices of power. To return to sexology then, as this special issue does, is to inquire into sexology's influence on the making of our present world and to theorize how it has given shape to some of the most vital questions central to gender and sexuality studies today: questions about how sciences of racialization begat—and continue to beget—understandings of gendered and sexual diversity and difference; about how these sciences fed modern-day legacies of eugenics and other biopolitical forms of population management; about how the relationship between gender and sexuality is theorized, by whom, and to what ends; about how a range of sciences responsible for biological accounts of gender difference, including but not limited to gynecology and endocrinology, insofar as they rely on specific forms of scientized bodily scrutiny, may or may not be drawing from sexological methods of investigation; and many more. While this special issue cannot comprehensively answer these questions, it *does* speak to the vast epistemological terrain and infrastructural landscape upon which sexological thought has left its mark and the pressing need for further examination of the long tail of these sciences and their effects.

As a part of our efforts to capture, or at least characterize, sexology's incredible handiness as a tool for state and nonstate discipline, we offer two methodologies for tracking sexual science: one spatial and infrastructural, and the other temporal. In the first of these, we take up and revamp the study of global sexology through what Ann Laura Stoler (2001: 831) calls "circuits of knowledge production," mapping the way that sexual science's squishiness richly capacitates it for movement and enables it to be ported and portable for uptake in a hugely various set of discursive sites. Stoler's methodology has led to a growing body of work tracing overlapping and interconnected circuitries of sexuality and sexological knowledge; the most well-mapped of these circuits is the so-called "Latin circuit."[5] This circuit of exchange encompassed France, Italy, Spain, Romance-speaking Switzerland, Portugal, Romania, Argentina, Mexico, Cuba, Brazil, Paraguay, Peru, Venezuela, and Chile, and was built on a shared cultural imaginary of Latinness "based on a synthesis of Ancient Roman civilization, linguistic and cultural commonality, and Roman Catholicism (in the Romanian case, Christian Orthodoxy)" (Turda and Gillette 2014: 1). Sexual knowledge moved between and was created in collaboration among these countries in rich, multidirectional circuits of transatlantic exchange. Our special issue implicitly builds on and critiques this methodology, drawing attention to the ways in which it tends to focus on majoritarian subjects in global capital cities or nation-states and thus struggles to account for minoritarian subjects and regional specificities. The essays that follow, and especially those by Zohar Weiman-Kelman, Howard Chiang, Rovel Sequeira, Aaron Stone, and Emmett Harsin Drager, embody a multivocal critique of this approach in method, content, and argument.

For example, Weiman-Kelman's essay, "Yiddish Sexology: A New Language for the History of Sexuality," approaches the well-known fact that many of the most influential European sexologists—including Heinrich Kaan, Iwan Bloch, Albert Moll, Marc André Raffalovich, Magnus Hirschfeld, Cesare Lombroso, Max Marcuse, and Ludwig Levi Lenz—were Jewish, and turns to Yiddish sexology to track "how European Jews theorized their own sex, in their own deviant tongue." Weiman-Kelman posits Yiddish as a linguistic circuit that operates outside nation-states and "national narrative[s]" of sexuality, given the uneven citizenship status of European Jewry and the transnational nature of Yiddish, a transnationality that—because it is produced in part in Europe—"challenges the dichotomous distinction between 'the west' and its 'others.'" This special issue is organized around precisely this kind of nuanced, grounded intellectual history, taking as a point of departure what Laura Doan (2019: 307–8) characterizes as global sexuality studies' "paramount interest in knowledge as it travels in multidirectional ways" and thus the fundamentally "dialogical nature" of epistemologies of sex.[6]

Howard Chiang's and Rovel Sequeira's essays further elaborate the theorization of the circuit by pointing to a vast Asian network of sexual scientific knowledge, which has thus far been overshadowed by the European-centered idea of the circuit itself. In the widespread global circulation of ideas, sexological study and practice took on a life of their own in Asia and were quickly absorbed by a wide range of both state and nonstate disciplinary formations, such as colonial and metropolitan law, medicine, and education. For instance, while German sexological materials flowed into Japan beginning around 1875, these materials were retrofitted into already-existing infrastructures of scientific exchange between Japan and China, through their collective grappling with this supposedly Western sexual science (Pflugfelder 1999; Driscoll 2005; Rocha 2010; Chiang 2018). At the same time, Japan disseminated its sexological ideas to its Korean colonies, while there was precious little at least acknowledged flow from Japanese, Chinese, or Korean sources back to Europe (Driscoll 2005: 223n36). Even as we know that major European figures in the history of sexology, such as Magnus Hirschfeld, did visit Japan and China, Hirschfeld's work neither cites nor seems to think with important Japanese sexologists such as Tanaka Kōgai, Habuto Eiji, or Sawada Junjirō, or Chinese sexologists such as Zhang Jingsheng, Pan Guangdan, or Chai Fuyuan. In this telling *lack* of a certain dialogism with non-European sexological traditions, European sexology begins to look less like a circuit than an echo chamber, suggesting the need for site-specific accounts of circulation that would offer rich cartographies of the movements of global sexual knowledge.

Chiang's essay, "The Secrets of a Loyalist Soul: Psychoanalysis and Homosexuality in Wartime China," offers such a geographically located account, taking up the example of Bingham Dai, a pathbreaking US American-trained Chinese psychoanalyst, to brilliantly theorize what he calls Dai's "transcultural style of reasoning," which foregrounds Chinese cultural knowledge and "debunks the assumption that Western biomedical categories are universally applicable." In so doing, Chiang sketches the way in which these flows of sexual science were not meant necessarily to circulate but rather to provide location-specific kinds of knowledge.

Similarly, Sequeira's "The Anatomy of Habit: Prison Sexology and the Scandal of Pederasty in Colonial India" illustrates the uneven flows of sexual knowledge, uncovering a hitherto unknown sex scandal in colonial Indian prisons. This essay examines the sexological study that John Mulvany, an Irish medical officer, conducted at the Alipore New Central Jail in the second decade of the twentieth century, as he tested British penological and sexological theories of the relationship between prison spatial relations and sodomy. The results of his study, however, were systematically ignored by both colonial administrators and those outside India. Sequeira uses Mulvany's study to illustrate how the colonial order was "produced through degrees of willful ignorance rather than through knowledge," indexing a heretofore understudied facet of the role of sexual science in the landscape of colonial power.

If the flows of sexological thought extended unevenly across the globe, they also tended to cluster around specific ideas, formations, and populations in particular regions. In the United States, as scholars such as Jules Gill-Peterson and Emma Heaney detail, the concentration of sexological sciences' disciplinary power tended to intensify in its interface with Black and Brown populations (Gill-Peterson and Heaney, in progress; Velocci 2021a). Indeed, one of the questions that joins a number of essays in this issue—including the aforementioned essays by Weiman-Kelman and Sequeira, but also those by Harsin Drager and Stone—is an inquiry into how race became the occasion for extensive theorizing about the significance of sexual comportment, morphology, and difference writ large, even as the increasing authoritativeness of the sexological sciences lent new force to extant and modernizing forms of racism.

For example, Harsin Drager's essay "Early Gender Clinics, Transsexual

Etiology, and the Racialized Family" charts how the clinical, sexological gaze that was believed to be directed nearly exclusively at white and Jewish subjects also encompasses Black people. The essay begins with a startling archival discovery: namely, that some of the first patients at the most storied early gender clinics were people of color "who made their way to the clinics via state psychiatric hospitals and/or the criminal justice system." Correcting earlier accounts of these clinics as populated by largely white and middle-class patients, Harsin Drager traces how "early transsexual research hinged on racialized patients and the pathologization of the racialized family, while simultaneously appearing to be raceless." In particular, they read the confluence of racial science and trans therapeutics in the work of Robert Stoller, John Money, and Daniel Patrick Moynihan to offer a new account of the racialized construction of mid-twentieth-century trans identity in the United States.

While Harsin Drager's account of sexology's role in the clinical practice of the first US American gender clinics further blurs an increasingly indistinct line between sexual science and scientific racism, Aaron Stone's essay approaches the question of how Black writers—many of whom were inspired by sexological writings—engaged with this archive despite its notably pernicious past and present. "Toward a Black Vernacular Sexology" reads across literary works by Pauline Hopkins, Sutton Griggs, Paul Lawrence Dunbar, and especially Charles Chesnutt to theorize how "Black modes of sexual knowledge production engaged with institutional sexology." In particular, Stone argues that Chesnutt's *The Marrow of Tradition* (1901) deploys a "black vernacular sexology" to undermine and reverse the racist presumptions of white sexology. That is, Chesnutt's work transforms its Black protagonists from, in the words of Weiman-Kelman, the "objects of [sexual] science to its producers." In this sense, both Stone's and Weiman-Kelman's essays trace how minoritized ethnic and racial communities fashion alternative and depathologized accounts of their sexual lives.

If one of the aspirations of this special issue is to chart the circulation of sexological thinking between global and regional networks, most of the essays that take up this challenge tend to focus on these flows across the first half of the twentieth century. So, lest we accommodate any sort of deeply erroneous suggestion that sexology is "over"—a vestige of past ways of thinking, an atavism that properly belongs to the decades prior to the apotheoses of various gendered and sexual liberation movements—the second guiding framework and method we brought to assembling this issue is what we call *present-tense sexual science*. This approach tries to capture the aliveness of sexology and sexological logics today. While the imbrication of sexological thinking within institutions and epistemes has been a feature of sexology's history since its inception, the project of tracing what Lubin and Vaccaro have termed sexology's "afterlives" has recently experienced something of a resurgence in a range of fields, among them transgender studies, Black studies, and critical ethnic studies. This perspective has emphasized sexology's character as both what Foucault has called a *dispositif* and as a method, a particular way of looking, analyzing, and consolidating information that "operationaliz[es] bodily difference as public policy and infrastructure" (Lubin and Vaccaro 2021: 5).

Rather than something that is *after* or undead, we understand sexual science as very much a part of contemporary self-making and understandings of identity. To this end, Kadji Amin's "Taxonomically Queer? Sexology and New Queer, Trans, and Asexual Identities" reveals the vitality of sexology's difficult-to-grasp contemporaneity, tracking vernacular sexual and gender identities in the present. This essay takes as its focus what Amin calls the "taxonomical renaissance" evident in our contemporary moment's "proliferation of genders and sexualities," as part of the essay's broader effort to trace this renaissance's sexological past and its relation to its legacies of racism and imperial violence. Amin's essay explores the affordances and pitfalls of such taxonomies and ultimately theorizes an ethical relation to their fraught pasts. In so doing, he animates the liveness of sexology as a form of sexual common sense and elucidates how its logics continue to reverberate in and shape the present.

The sheer cultural and epistemological *endurance* of sexological logics also throbs in the contemporary debates around the so-called gay gene, as Stephanie Clare, Patrick R. Grzanka, and Joanna Wuest demonstrate in their contribution, "Gay Genes in the Postgenomic Era: A Roundtable." This roundtable offers a collective exploration of the cultural consequences of Ganna et al.'s 2019 Genome Wide Association Study, lauded as perhaps the most technologically advanced sexual scientific inquiry ever undertaken, but whose results were yawned at as being "unsurprising and unremarkable" insofar as the study found that "genes contribute minimally, inconsistently, and complexly to human sexual expression." Grzanka's contribution to the roundtable, "Programs of Life/Knowing Ourselves," offers an ethnography of Ganna et al.'s study, theorizing its cultural reception to recover the contemporary "*affective investment* in bioessentialism" that the study indexes. Wuest, too, takes up the durability of sexual biologisms in her essay, "The Dream of Bioessentialism Is Alive in a Postgenomic Era," in which she historicizes the rise of bioessentialism, reading the emergence of the putative "gay gene" in light of "political economic and legal incentives." Finally, Stephanie Clare's "Biological Sex and the 'Overrepresentation of Man'" identifies the racial history of the notion of "same-sexness" that lends the Ganna study its epistemological foundations, exposing how the study reifies dimorphic constructions of sex and shores up a universalizing logic that assumes and thus prioritizes whiteness. Together these contributions make evident how much sexology continues to inform pervasive understandings of sex and gender.

The frameworks we have elaborated here—thinking with the global circulation of sexological thought and its particularized efflorescence in specific regional circuits, on the one hand, and thinking with the sexual sciences of the present, on the other—cut a starkly different figure from older and more traditional approaches to sexological intellectual histories, like the "great man" model that focuses on a single figure, or scholarship that focuses on particular sexual formations (notably, homosexuality and inversion). Because we agree with Kirsten Leng and Katie Sutton's (2021: 4) contention that "the historiography of sexology is young"—and, we would add, full of possibility—we want to conclude by gesturing toward a few more of the methodological openings that the essays collected here afford. Developing a thick, critical relationship to the histories and presents of the sexological is important because sexology is not a dismissible object. If we have learned anything from curating this special issue, it is that the sexological sciences have had a profoundly long reach and a surprisingly enduring impact on people and knowledge systems all over the world. Sexology has, at its best, a complex and profoundly ambivalent history, and for every person who has identified something salutary in its insights—and it is no coincidence that many who have are white and from the global North—there are scores of others who have encountered it through the vagaries of state discipline: the prison, the hospital, the law. In the context of many major US gendered and sexual cultures—both those that are more normative and those that are more minoritarian (and which can often be normative in their own ways)—there is not really an escape hatch out of the reach of sexological logics; one cannot really opt out. Indeed, as Amin argues in this special issue, even those who seek to renounce gender (i.e., people identifying as *agender*) or sexual identity still announce these refusals in a taxonomical idiom that is nearly impossible to divorce from the history of sexual and gender classifications, which are themselves also legacies of the sexological. We thus conclude in a more theoretical tenor, asking: how do we cultivate a critical—dare we say *ethical*?—relationship to sexology's legacies? Insofar as it is difficult, in many contexts, to describe gendered or sexual experience or identification in a way that eludes sexology's epistemological capture, how do we reckon with the complex and deeply compromised quality of not only these vocabularies' distant histories, but also their pressing *presents*? We hope this special issue offers a blueprint for readers grappling with these questions, and many others.

Notes

1. The recent attention and renewed interest in these archives are evident in books like Snorton 2017, Heaney 2017, Gill-Peterson 2018, LaFleur 2018, Kahan 2019, See 2020, and Chiang 2021.

2. For an account of the relation between "It" and sexual allure, see Roach 2007. Our title is also, in part, inspired by Richardson 2013.

3. For a debate on the definition of sexology, see Crozier and Bauer 2017.

4. On the relation between sexology and nonhuman animals, see Linge 2021 and Velocci 2021b. We would be excited to follow Linge and Velocci in thinking sexual science outside the human into teratology or to explore Erasmus Darwin's *The Loves of the Plants* (1789), Eugen Steinach's work with rats, Serge Voronoff's work with monkeys, Richard B. Goldschmidt's lepidopterology, and Auguste Forel's theorization of ants and other insects.

5. On a circuit-based approach, see Fuechtner, Haynes, and Jones 2018. On the Latin circuit, see, e.g., Cleminson 2009, Turda and Gillette 2014, Cleminson 2016, Jones 2018, Beccalossi 2018, MacMillan 2018, and Beccalossi 2021. This body of work has its intellectual roots in Stepan 1991. For alternative methodologies and conceptualizations for theorizing transnational and global sexuality, see Canaday 2009, Bauer 2015, and Kahan 2017.

6. The scholarly texts that Doan describes as most clearly exemplifying this circuit model are Bauer 2015 and Fuechtner, Haynes, and Jones 2018.

References

Bauer, Heike. 2015. *Sexology and Translation: Cultural and Scientific Encounters across the Modern World*. Philadelphia, PA: Temple University Press.

Beccalossi, Chiara. 2018. "Latin Eugenics and Sexual Knowledge in Italy, Spain, and Argentina: International Networks across the Atlantic." In *A Global History of Sexual Science*, edited by Veronika Fuechtner, Douglas E. Haynes, and Ryan M. Jones, 305–29. Berkeley: University of California Press.

Beccalossi, Chiara. 2021. "Types, Norms, and Normalization: Hormone Research and Treatments in Italy, Argentina, and Brazil, c. 1900–1950." *History of the Human Sciences* 34, no. 2: 113–37.

Bull, Sarah. 2021. "More Than a Case of Mistaken Identity: Adult Entertainment and the Making of Early Sexology." *History of the Human Sciences* 34, no. 1: 10–39.

Canaday, Margot, ed. 2009. "*AHR* Forum: Transnational Sexualities." *American Historical Review* 114, no. 5: 1250–1353.

Chiang, Howard. 2018. *After Eunuchs: Science, Medicine, and the Transformation of Sex in Modern China*. New York: Columbia University Press.

Chiang, Howard. 2021. *Transtopia in the Sinophone Pacific*. New York: Columbia University Press.

Cleminson, Richard. 2009. "Transnational Discourse on the 'Male Vida': Male Homosexuality in Madrid, Buenos Aires, and Barcelona in the Early Twentieth Century." *Journal of Spanish Cultural Studies* 10, no. 4: 461–83.

Cleminson, Richard. 2016. "Between Germanic and Latin Eugenics: Portugal, 1930–1960." *História, Ciências, Saúde–Manguinhos* 23, no. 1: 73–91.

Cocks, H. G. 2004. "Saucy Stories: Pornography, Sexology, and the Marketing of Sexual Knowledge in Britain c. 1918–70." *Social History* 29, no. 4: 465–84.

Crozier, Ivan, and Heike Bauer. 2017. "Sexology, Historiography, Citation, Embodiment: A Review and (Frank) Exchange." *History of the Human Sciences*, June 27. http://www.histhum.com/?p=367.

Dixon, Joy. 1997. "Sexology and the Occult: Sexuality and Subjectivity in Theosophy's New Age." *Journal of the History of Sexuality* 7, no. 3: 409–33.

Doan, Laura. 2019. "Troubling Popularisation: On the Gendered Circuits of a 'Scientific' Knowledge of Sex." *Gender and History* 31, no. 2: 307–8.

Driscoll, Mark. 2005. "Seeds and (Nest) Eggs of Empire: Sexology Manuals/Manual Sexology." In *Gendering Modern Japanese History*, edited by Cathleen Uno and Barbara Maloney, 191–224. Cambridge, MA: Harvard University Press.

Ferguson, Roderick. 2004. *Aberrations in Black: Toward a Queer of Color Critique*. Minneapolis: University of Minnesota Press.

Fuechtner, Veronika, Douglas E. Haynes, and Ryan M. Jones. 2018. "Introduction: Toward a Global History of Sexual Science: Movements, Networks, and Deployments." In *A Global History of Sexual Science*, edited by Veronika Fuechtner, Douglas E. Haynes, and Ryan M. Jones, 1–25. Berkeley: University of California Press.

Ganna, Andrea, et al. 2019. "Large-Scale GWAS Reveals Insights into the Genetic Architecture of Same-Sex Sexual Behavior." *Science* 365, no. 6456. https://www.science.org/doi/10.1126/science.aat7693.

Gill-Peterson, Jules. 2018. *Histories of the Transgender Child*. Minneapolis: University of Minnesota Press.

Gill-Peterson, Jules, and Emma Heaney. In progress. "The Ghost Cousins."

Heaney, Emma. 2017. *The New Woman: Literary Modernism, Queer Theory, and the Trans Feminine Allegory*. Evanston, IL: Northwestern University Press.

Irvine, Janice. 2005. *Disorders of Desire: Sexuality and Gender in Modern American Sexology*. Philadelphia, PA: Temple University Press.

Jones, Ryan M. 2018. "Mexican Sexology and Male Homosexuality: Genealogies and

Global Contexts, 1860–1957." In *A Global History of Sexual Science*, edited by Veronika Fuechtner, Douglas E. Haynes, and Ryan M. Jones, 232–57. Berkeley: University of California Press.

Kahan, Benjamin. 2017. "Conjectures on the Sexual World-System." *GLQ* 23, no. 3: 327–57.

Kahan, Benjamin. 2019. *The Book of Minor Perverts: Sexology, Etiology, and the Emergences of Sexuality*. Chicago: University of Chicago Press.

LaFleur, Greta. 2018. *The Natural History of Sexuality in Early America*. Baltimore, MD: Johns Hopkins University Press.

Leng, Kirsten, and Katie Sutton. 2021. "Histories of Sexology Today: Reimagining the Boundaries of *Scientia Sexualis*." *History of the Human Sciences* 34, no. 1: 3–9.

Linge, Ina. 2021. "The Potency of the Butterfly: The Reception of Richard B. Goldschmidt's Animal Experiments in German Sexology around 1920." *History of the Human Sciences* 34, no. 1: 40–70.

Lubin, Joan, and Jeanne Vaccaro. 2021. "After Sexology." *Social Text* 39, no. 3 (148): 1–16.

MacMillan, Kurt. 2018. "'Forms So Attenuated That They Merge into Normality Itself': Alexander Lipschütz, Gregorio Marañón, and Theories of Intersexuality in Chile, Circa 1930." In *A Global History of Sexual Science*, edited by Veronika Fuechtner, Douglas E. Haynes, and Ryan M. Jones, 330–52. Berkeley: University of California Press.

Pflugfelder, Gregory. 1999. *Cartographies of Desire: Male-Male Sexuality in Japanese Discourse, 1600–1900*. Berkeley: University of California Press.

Richardson, Sarah S. 2013. *Sex Itself: The Search for Male and Female in the Human Genome*. Chicago: University of Chicago Press.

Roach, Joseph. 2007. *It*. Ann Arbor: University of Michigan Press.

Rocha, Leon Antonio. 2010. "*Xing*: The Discourse of Sex and Human Nature in Modern China." *Gender and History* 22, no. 3: 603–28.

Rubin, Gayle. 2012. "Thinking Sex: Notes for a Radical Theory of the Politics of Sexuality." In *Deviations: A Gayle Rubin Reader*, 137–81. Durham, NC: Duke University Press.

See, Sam. 2020. *Queer Natures, Queer Mythologies*, edited by Christopher Looby and Michael North. New York: Fordham University Press.

Snorton, C. Riley. 2017. *Black on Both Sides: A Racial History of Trans Identity*. Minneapolis: University of Minnesota Press.

Stepan, Nancy Leys. 1991. *"The Hour of Eugenics": Race, Gender, and Nation in Latin America*. Ithaca, NY: Cornell University Press.

Stoler, Ann Laura. 2001. "Tense and Tender Ties." *Journal of American History* 88, no. 3: 829–65.

Turda, Marius, and Aaron Gillette. 2014. *Latin Eugenics in a Comparative Perspective*. London: Bloomsbury.

Velocci, Beans. 2021a. "Binary Logic: Race, Expertise, and the Persistence of Uncertainty in American Sex Research." PhD diss., Yale University.

Velocci, Beans. 2021b. "Sex and the Species: Making Human Meaning of Animal Bodies at Cold Spring Harbor Eugenics Laboratories." March 10. https://www.sciencehistory.org/event/lunchtime-lecture-beans-velocci.

Wolffram, Heather. 2009. *The Stepchildren of Science: Psychical Research and Parapsychology in Germany, c. 1870–1939*. Amsterdam: Rodopi.

EARLY GENDER CLINICS, TRANSSEXUAL ETIOLOGY, AND THE RACIALIZED FAMILY

Emmett Harsin Drager

On June 12, 1966, *The National Insider* ran an article titled "I Ruined My Life When I Changed Sex" (Gould 1966). The article details the life of jazz singer Delisa Newton, often referred to as the subject of the "first Negro sex change." In the interview, Newton explains the hurdles that prevented many people of her day from being able to access trans therapeutics. She states: "There are tough state laws against sex change surgery, unless detailed psychiatric examination shows it to be necessary. In my case, three years of psychiatric sessions and an additional 10 months as a psychiatric hospital patient convinced the doctors I should be transformed into a woman physically. The operations were done at a university medical school here in California. It was perfectly legal and perfectly successful."

Newton's story first broke a year earlier in another *National Insider* article. Newton received sex reassignment surgery sometime before 1965; if the information she provided about her psychiatric care in this interview is accurate, one can assume she began pursuing medical transition sometime around 1960. This raises the question of where exactly Newton received treatment. Between 1960 and 1965, not a single California university was publicly operating a gender clinic that offered surgical intervention for transsexual patients.[1]

A copy of this article is held in the Robert J. Stoller Papers in Special Collections at the UCLA Library. On the yellow, faded newspaper clipping, someone has used a ballpoint pen to mark annotations in blue ink. The markings bracket the above quoted section, with an arrow pointing to the words "university medical center here in California" (see fig. 1). Was Newton a patient at UCLA? How did she

GLQ 29:1
DOI 10.1215/10642684-10144364
© 2023 by Duke University Press

Figure 1. Photograph of Delissa Newton from a
June 12, 1966, article in *The National Insider*.
Photograph from the Robert Stoller Papers in
UCLA Library Special Collections.

First Negro Sex Change

I never dreamed I would have so much grief, says Delissa.

get there? What was her path from inpa-
tient psychiatric care to a groundbreaking
(and secret) medical operation at a pre-
mier university hospital?

The first university-based gender
clinics operated in the United States from
the early 1960s to approximately 1980.[2]
During this two-decade period, doctors and researchers would attempt to find a
cause and a psychiatric treatment (i.e., a cure) for transsexuality. They would ultimately fail in this search for an etiology and would move toward surgical and hormonal treatments. The university-based gender clinics were responsible for craft-
ing the diagnosis of gender identity disorder and the treatment protocols known as
the Standards of Care, which still shape trans therapeutics to this day.

While Newton may have figured as an exceptional case in the US media, it
is likely that many individuals have stories that mirror hers. In this article, I argue
that in the early days of university gender research in the United States, there were
many patients who made their way to the clinics via state psychiatric hospitals
and/or the criminal justice system. These patients, often people of color with stories similar to Newton's, provided the foundation for early theories of transsexual
etiology. Their stories foreground how psychiatric detention and unfreedom were
necessary conditions for the production of modern sex and gender.

I examine the research and writing of UCLA gender-clinic practitioner
Robert J. Stoller alongside the work of US senator and sociologist Daniel Patrick
Moynihan and his famous essay "The Negro Family: The Case for National Action"
(1965). I put these mid-twentieth-century thinkers into conversation to highlight
the racial and colonial logics of the university-based gender clinics and their significance for transsexual life (both then and now). Stoller, the preeminent thinker
on psychiatric theories of trans etiology, and Moynihan theorized gender pathology
as a multigenerational process and problem, understanding treatment to extend
beyond the individual and into the family structure and culture more broadly.

In this article I aim to make three things clear. First, gender-clinic patients
were not all white and middle class, and many of them did not come to the gender
clinics voluntarily. Some clinic patients were ensnarled in the criminal justice sys-

tem and/or involuntarily detained in psychiatric facilities. Second, understanding the prolonged, multigenerational temporality of Stoller's theory of transsexual etiology makes clear the connections between transsexual medicine, evolutionary and eugenic theory, and racial science. And third, that Stoller's theory of transsexual etiology emerges alongside essays like Moynihan's reveals the shared genealogy of US sexology and Jim Crow. These interventions are critical for trans studies' material understanding of the shared histories of trans medicine and racial subjugation.

Racing for an Etiology

In 1977, Dr. Donald Laub, the chief of plastic surgery at Stanford University School of Medicine, delivered a public lecture about the cause and treatments of transsexualism.[3] In the talk, Laub outlined two currents of thought that attempt to explain the etiology of transsexualism: hormones before birth and social environment after birth. Laub proceeded to describe a study carried out in Boston on a cohort of diabetic women and their sons. These women, who had problems carrying a child to full term, were given high doses of "female hormones" in an attempt to prevent miscarriages. Eighteen years later, professors of psychiatry at Stanford University studied their sons. They wanted to examine whether these boys, who had been exposed to high levels of "female hormones" in utero, were more likely to be homosexual or transsexual.

To perform this double-blind study, the Stanford psychiatry professors had the boys hit baseballs with a bat and field ground balls. They recorded the participants doing these athletic acts to determine whether these subjects were more effeminate than "normal" boys. They also interviewed the participants and their mothers. According to their analysis, the results were mixed. They argued that these boys were far more effeminate than their peers but that none of them were homosexual nor transsexual. Laub uses this study as a means to suggest that the cause of transsexuality is "probably a combination" of hormones and environment.

At the time he delivered this lecture in 1977, Laub was considered a leading expert in transsexuality. What this lecture demonstrates is that even those who were deemed to be "experts" had little to no idea what caused transsexuality. To use a baseball metaphor, they were pitchers unable to find the strike zone, batters who couldn't get on base; they were doctors trying to treat a problem they knew very little about. As Harry Benjamin (1966: 5) writes: "Ordinarily, the purpose of scientific investigation is to bring more clarity, more light into fields of obscurity. Modern researchers, however, delving into 'the riddle of sex,' have actually produced— so far—more obscurity, more complexity." Throughout the century, ideas about "true sex" would proliferate; however, research tended to complicate rather than clarify.[4]

Racelessness and the Carceral Clinic

Transgender studies scholars such as Dan Irving, Dean Spade, and Aren Aizura have pointed to the ways in which transsexual narratives and diagnostic criteria demand a certain type of patient—one capable of meeting standards of productivity and success under racial capitalism (Irving 2013; Spade 2006; Aizura 2018). The clinics' criteria for surgery always favored white and/or middle-class patients. I do not dispute these scholars, but I do add a caveat to their analysis. By looking at the patients who were seen *before* surgical and hormonal interventions became the norm, we find a cohort of patients of color who were sought out by gender-clinic doctors because of the idea that gender deviance was hyperpresent in racialized populations and family structures. This article is concerned with the ways in which early transsexual research hinged on racialized patients and the pathologization of the racialized family, while simultaneously appearing to be raceless.

In a report titled "Case History Data from 392 Male and 71 Female Transsexuals," Dr. Harry Benjamin, his secretary Virginia Allen, and psychologist Stanley Krippner assembled a comprehensive survey of transsexuals seeking treatment at gender clinics. Their report pulled from the largest patient sample size of any study at the time. Published in October 1973, the report carefully outlines the patients' demographic and background information, including age, occupation, religious background, socioeconomic background, educational background, first occurrence of cross-dressing, frequency of cross-dressing, sexual activity, number on the Kinsey scale, attitudes of parents and spouses, parents' marital status, siblings, siblings' marital status, therapy history, previous neurological diagnoses, pertinent medical operations and treatments, substance use, veteran status, and history of masturbation. From this list we can see how the data they collected on each individual was extensive. In the quest to understand the etiology of transsexuality there was no stone left unturned, except for what is glaringly missing from this list: race.

During this period the omission of race also took the form of excision. In 1973, for example, Stoller published *Splitting: A Case of Female Masculinity*. The book is based on years of therapy with a transmasculine patient, referred to by the pseudonym Mrs. G. Mrs. G is described on the first page of *Splitting* as "a white, divorced housewife in her thirties, living in a suburb of Los Angeles with two teenage sons" (Stoller 1997: 1). In correspondence between Stoller and his book editor,

Emanuel Geltman, there is a short but seismic postscript: "You never mentioned that her mother was Mexican—something she refers to in this morning's letter."[5] Geltman, who had begun writing letters with Mrs. G to receive her consent for the book's publication, was pressing Stoller as to why he never mentioned her Latinidad anywhere in the manuscript. In his reply Stoller writes: "Finally, in reply to your P.S. about her mother being Mexican, I did not realize that there was no mention of this whatsoever, for it shows up throughout the transcripts that she speaks Spanish and has [a] Mexican background. In fact, her mother is a very atypical Chicano [*sic*] indeed, so much so that it would confuse the reader if she were so described. So the saga unfolds."[6] Indeed, it is impossible to know what exactly Stoller meant by "atypical Chicano," but it raises a series of questions. First, what about her ethnicity would be confusing to readers? If the mother were a "typical" Chicana would it be deemed necessary to mention her ethnicity? Was this omission in fact accidental? Despite Stoller's claim that he did not realize he had failed to mention her Latinidad, he goes on to justify its omission.

Splitting sensationalizes Mrs. G's criminality and run-ins with the law. She's a serial criminal who has been arrested for car theft, check fraud, and homicidal thoughts. From Stoller's personal papers we can also learn that she was forcefully sterilized by the state and was required by the court to see a therapist.[7] Stoller first met Mrs. G in a Los Angeles County hospital where he had gone to film interviews with psychiatric patients to use for medical students' clinical evaluations. He describes Mrs. G's transfer to UCLA as follows: "She asked if she could be transferred to UCLA Hospital for treatment; she feared her path from the county hospital would lead back to the hospital from which she had run away and to the unavailing experiences she had had in the past with state hospitals" (Stoller 1997: 12). This information tells us a very different history of transsexual medicine. In addition to Mrs. G's identity throwing into question the ubiquitous assumption that early clinic patients were white and middle class, Mrs. G's status as a recipient of court-mandated treatment also teaches us something about the (in)voluntary status of some gender-clinic patients. While Mrs. G requested to be transferred to UCLA, it was from the position of a person ensnarled in the criminal justice and state hospital system.

Mrs. G is not the only patient who challenges received narratives of gender-clinic patients. In an undated report from the University of Michigan Gender Identity Clinic (GIC) titled "Varieties of Male Transsexualism," there is a short footnote about the cases being examined.[8] It reads: "Age and racial data on the patients: Case 1: 26 y.o. Negro; Case 2: 25 y.o. Negro; Case 3: 22 y.o. White; Case 4: 29 y.o. White; Case 5: 26 y.o. Negro; Case 6: 26 y.o. Negro." This data is noteworthy. Of the six patients being closely examined and quoted in the report, four of them are Black.

The GIC was founded in 1968 in the university medical school's Department of Obstetrics and Gynecology. The clinic worked closely with faculty in urology, plastic surgery, and psychiatry to focus on "sex alteration of selected individuals who are unhappy with their now gender role and cannot be treated by the usual methods" (Stern 2015: 61). The department recruited many of its patients from Wayne County General Hospital (WCGH) in the metropolitan Detroit area. WCGH, also known as Eloise Psychiatric Hospital, opened in the early nineteenth century as a sanatorium and poorhouse. For years it was the largest psychiatric hospital in the United States.

At the time that the clinic was founded, J. Robert Wilson was chair of the OB-GYN department. During his time as chair, he was invested in the University of Michigan's medical school strengthening their ties to WCGH, a relationship he viewed as "particularly valuable because of the volume of indigent patients with many serious complications of pregnancy which are seldom seen in Ann Arbor" (Stern 2015: 36). Not long after Wilson arrived at Michigan in 1964 and ramped up recruitment from WCGH, the GIC was founded. The Michigan clinic's connection with WCGH in metro Detroit might help explain the patient demographic data in the "Varieties of Male Transsexualism" report. Like Mrs. G and Delisa Newton, these case histories may have been collected from psychiatric patients.

According to trans elder Miss Major, in the 1950s and 1960s people who were arrested under cross-dressing laws were commonly sent to psychiatric facilities rather than jails, a situation she found herself in multiple times (Griffin-Gracy 2017). Their detentions were involuntary.[9] Gender-clinic doctors and researchers would visit these facilities looking for potential research subjects, just as Stoller had done when he encountered Mrs. G, or as Wilson advocated for during his tenure as chair of the OB-GYN department. State psychiatric hospitals were fertile ground for the recruitment of patients with conditions deemed to be unique or complicated. In Mrs. G's case, she asked to be transferred from a state psychiatric hospital to the UCLA gender clinic, seeing it as a potentially more benevolent or therapeutic option. It's unclear whether all gender-clinic patients from psychiatric facilities consented to their transfer like Mrs. G, or if some became objects of research without a say in the matter. Without more case histories it is hard to draw a conclusion. However, from the records available, there is an obvious linkage between the university-based gender-clinic research and the prevalence of involuntary psychiatric treatment in midcentury trans communities.

Mother Theory

On September 20, 1966, at around four in the afternoon, Stoller entered the Roosevelt Hotel in Hollywood, California, to meet with Dr. Harry Benjamin. Benjamin had just published his groundbreaking book *The Transsexual Phenomenon*. Despite Benjamin's years of clinical practice with transsexual patients, he had been unable to determine the cause of transsexuality. Stoller wanted to meet with Benjamin to get his perspective on his own nascent theory of transsexual etiology: the theory of too much mother. The theory was based on the notion that a mother who was too close to her child—shared too much intimacy, coddled too much—was the cause of effeminacy in young boys.[10] This mother, in conjunction with an absent or indifferent father, was enough to push a child to adult transsexualism. While Stoller was basing this theory on his clinical work with only three patients, he was quite excited about its potential for providing a theory of transsexuality in general.[11]

Using John Money's research on intersex children as a kind of control, Stoller set out to study individuals who, despite having no known biological cause for gender confusion, had developed an abnormal gender identity. If good parenting could ensure an intersex child a happy and normal life, then surely bad parenting was to blame for pathological gender deviance in non-intersex children. Adapting Money's term "gender role," Stoller (1968: 10) began to interrogate the source of what he called "gender identity," that is, "the knowledge and awareness, whether conscious or unconscious, that one belongs to one sex and not the other."

In 1968, Stoller published his seminal text *Sex and Gender: On the Development of Masculinity and Femininity*. Based on clinical research with adult and child transsexuals, their mothers, and in some cases their fathers, Stoller's central argument was that gender is "primarily culturally determined; that is, learned postnatally" and that the two main factors that impact this cultural process are one's society and one's mother (xiii).

Stoller develops a clinical picture of the type of mothering that leads to such gender confusion:

> This remarkable identification with women was found in these little boys to
> be associated with (1) mothers who acted and dressed like boys until adolescence; (2) fathers who were almost literally absent from the home, day or
> night, weekdays or weekends; (3) the parents' excessive permissiveness, so
> that the developing femininity was openly encouraged by allowing the boys
> to dress as girls whenever they chose ("He's so beautiful; wouldn't he look

lovely as a girl?") and especially by (4) excessive and intimate body contact for many hours, day and night, from birth to the time they were seen at age 4–5, this delay in mother-infant separation perpetuated by the little boys' constant touching of their mothers' nude bodies and clothes. (126–27)

Central to this theory is the idea that too much mother prevents her child from differentiating and developing a sense of self distinct and separate from her.[12] Stoller's theory explicitly connects such mothering to "primitive societies."[13] Turning to anthropological studies, Stoller outlines what mothering looks like in "primitive societies" in which "mother and infant are in a happy, skin-to-skin contact for many hours of the day and night, and for years, even to the extent that the child urinates and defecates unmolested on its mother's body" (106). Stoller suggests that there is not enough data to know if this primitive mothering leads to primitive gender deviance, suggesting that perhaps one key difference is that his subjects are isolated within the home, while in primitive societies "they are in the midst of the bustle of the community life" (107). In this section, Stoller finds a way of connecting pathological mothering to primitive or racialized mothering, a connection that unfolds below the surface of his research despite the preface claiming that "this research lacks controls from other cultures. My patients have been primarily white, middle-class Americans" (xiv).

Strikingly, Stoller's mother theory unfolds in time, requiring multiple generations of pathology before manifesting as adult transsexualism. According to Stoller, a young transsexual boy develops his gender deviance from having a mother who will not allow him to separate. This overbearing mother clings to her child because in her own childhood she had a mother who was indifferent to her. In *Sex and Gender*, the maternal grandmother is described as "empty." She is disinterested in her daughter and cannot give her the love she seeks. This experience of having an absent mother is what leads the daughter to become an overbearing mother for her transsexual son. Because her own mother was absent and empty, she may have sought validation from her father, which led to its own kind of gender pathology: tomboyishness and bisexuality. In this clinical picture, transsexuality is not an individual illness but rather a familial pathology that plays out over many generations.

To locate the etiology of transsexualism in many generations of pathological parenting is to extend the timeline of the development outside the window of postnatal life and into a longer, more evolutionary scale. An absent mother creates a masculine (gender deviant) daughter who, seeking to create the maternal connection that she was denied, coddles and smothers her son so much that he becomes a transsexual. Transsexualism is the result of unfit people procreating over many generations. This eugenic theory of gender pathology finds the cause of gender deviance to be a societal problem. In addition to extending the timeline of gender deviance, it also expands the unit of pathology/treatment beyond the individual and even the nuclear family, into many generations of the family.

Thinking about deviance in multigenerational or evolutionary terms is embedded in many aspects of sexology. In Sigmund Freud's (2014) *Three Essays on the Theory of Sexuality*, he argues that human life begins as anatomically bisexual—with bisexual referring to blurred sex characteristics rather than multiple-gender attraction—and moves toward one sex over the course of fetal development. Similarly, according to evolutionary theory, life begins as less sexually differentiated, and as a species evolves, so do two distinct sexes: male and female. As Siobhan Somerville (2000: 29) writes: "One of the basic assumptions within the Darwinian model was the belief that, as organisms evolved through a process of natural selection, they also showed greater signs of sexual differentiation."

In *Histories of the Transgender Child*, Jules Gill-Peterson (2018: 47–49) writes about G. Stanley Hall's theory of adolescence in order to draw out the similarities between ideas of individual/childhood development and evolutionary/societal development. When Hall created the category of the adolescent he saw it as the individual example of a preevolutionary stage, similar to the ways in which Enlightenment thinkers saw colonial countries and peoples as unevolved societies, the living history of present-day Europeans. As Gill-Peterson notes, "Growth was coded as unidirectional *and* parallel, at the individual and species level, binding childhood to a highly charged evolutionary concept of race as inheritable phenotype" (47). Hall's theories of the plasticity of the child mirrored the plasticity of a population, both of which were in need of a particular kind of cultivation. Perhaps what is most crucial is that Hall believed that improper childhood development—or, that is, arrested development—led to perversion. In this sense we can see how Stoller's theory of the overbearing mother is very much aligned with not only adolescent development but also ideas about evolution, eugenics, race, and coloniality.

The Pathologization of the Racialized Family

Three years prior to Stoller publishing *Sex and Gender*, another study about pathological parenting was released: Daniel Patrick Moynihan's "The Negro Family: The Case for National Action" (Moynihan 1965). Moynihan's thesis was that, while the civil rights movement demanded equality, equality would be impossible until the Black community adopted white European structures of the nuclear family with a male patriarch. "In essence," Moynihan writes, "the Negro community has been forced into a matriarchal structure which, because it is so out of line with the rest of American society, seriously retards the progress of the group as a whole" (29). He attributes generational poverty, delinquency, addiction, and a myriad of other social ills all to the problem of the Negro family, or more specifically, a matriarchal and dominant mother figure.

In Moynihan's report, the Black family structure is pathological because of its deviance from gender norms: "A fundamental fact of Negro family life is the often reversed roles of husband and wife" (30). In Black households, he argues, family pathology exists because of deviant gender roles. In the case of the transsexual, deviant gender identity exists because of family pathology. These are two sides of the same coin—an attempt to attribute social problems to a particular type of family. It is a pathology that builds across generations and is able to survive because of a perverse society that allows such pathology to germinate, something Moynihan attributes to social welfare programs that have allowed the Black matriarchal family structure to continue despite its "unnaturalness." In both Moynihan's and Stoller's theories of gender deviance and family pathology, the problem develops over generations, taking years to fully manifest. This process not only takes time but also requires the permissiveness and complicity of a society not intervening. The message is clear: gender deviance is to blame for social ills, social ills come from the family, and the family is corrupted by gender deviance.

While Stoller's work never cites or references the Moynihan report directly, it is important to understand these studies as emanating from the same therapeutic milieu: the rise of family therapy in the 1950s and 1960s. Under the family therapy model, pathology shifted from the individual to the family. The family unit was to blame for fascism, homosexuality, delinquency, and schizophrenia. As Deborah Weinstein (2013: 8) argues, the family became central to understanding "the etiology of mental illness." Understanding Stoller's theory of transsexual etiology as a multigenerational family pathology and as a by-product of the midcentury rise of family therapy and the expertise of psychological professionals provides a bridge toward understanding how trans therapeutics are intimately linked with theories of racialized family pathology.

An illustrative example of etiologies of gender difference and theories of family pathology crisscrossing in the gender clinics can be found in Money and Geoffrey Hosta's 1968 article "Negro Folklore of Male Pregnancy." The article tells of a myth about male pregnancy that the authors found circulating around Baltimore's homosexual community while conducting "a longitudinal study of problems in juvenile gender identity" (Money and Hosta 1968: 34). The myth of male pregnancy held that after being penetrated during anal sex, one could become pregnant with a "blood baby" if the sperm was able to travel deep into the anus and reach internal organs. Money's sample size for the paper was five individuals. In the discussion, the authors attribute this piece of folklore to the Negro family structure:

> Since it is a Negro phenomenon, one may look to the dynamics of Negro social and family life for a possible explanation of the viability of the folklore. The American Negro family, especially at the lower socio-economic level, is commonly mother-centered (and grandmother-centered). The father may be completely absent or a periodic visitor. In such a family framework, there might be considerable predisposition to encourage the maintenance and transmission of a tradition attributing maternal reproductive powers to the male. Perhaps the adolescent Negro boy, used to identifying with and imitating his mother . . . does not find so strange the idea that some of the physical aspects of motherhood may be assumed by a man. (48–49)

In this particular case, a study of juvenile gender identity problems in Baltimore's Black community led to a research paper on the folklore of male pregnancy. This folklore was attributed to the Negro family structure, which is deemed to be pathological. Money and Hosta's article highlights the Möbius strip nature of theories of gender perversity and pathological, racialized kinship structures—they feed off one another with no clear beginning or end.

It's also important to accentuate the fact that Money and Hosta's research on juvenile gender identity took them out into the streets of Black Baltimore, where the oral history of this myth of male pregnancy was gathered. Much like the data from the University of Michigan's GIC and the revelation that Mrs. G was Latina, this study points to the fact that in the early days of the gender clinic, racialized patient populations provided the foundation for theories of transsexual etiology. Because families of color, and most specifically Black families, were seen as being hotbeds of gender deviance, they provided fertile ground for researching the cause of such deviance. Highlighting the similarities between Stoller, Moynihan, and Money's work and the midcentury rise in psychiatric theories of family-caused pathology thus accentuates the relationship between the development of trans therapeutics and US racial science.

Notes

1. Stanford's clinic, often referred to as the first sex change clinic on the West Coast, would not officially announce its surgical program until 1969, with its first surgery performed in December 1968. Donald R. Laub to Spyros Andreopolous, November 13, 1968, folder 1, Donald R. Laub collection, Medical History Center, Lane Library, Stanford University, Stanford, CA.

2. As Jules Gill-Peterson (2018) notes in her book *Histories of the Transgender Child*, Johns Hopkins Hospital opened Brady Urological Institute in 1915, where Hugh Hampton Young treated intersex patients, especially children from the pediatric Harriet Lane Home. Similarly, doctors at UCLA treated intersex patients before the official launch of the Gender Identity Research Clinic, most notably the case of Agnes Torres. However, these clinics only saw patients that they deemed to have an intersex condition and not transsexuality (although the two categories often commingled in theory and practice).

3. Donald Laub public lecture, 1977, box 5, Meyer Library Lecture Tapes, Archive of Recorded Sound, Stanford University, Stanford, CA.

4. "True sex" is an epistemological category masquerading as an ontological category. "True sex" is based on the assumption that despite the various components that make up the sexed body (hormones, chromosomes, primary and secondary sex characteristics), each individual has a true, binaristic sex (male or female) that can be determined using empirical science and medicine.

5. Emanuel Geltman to Robert Stoller, February 2, 1972, box 32, Robert J. Stoller Papers, Library Special Collections, Charles E. Young Research Library, UCLA.

6. Robert Stoller to Emanuel Geltman, February 7, 1972, box 32, Robert J. Stoller Papers, Library Special Collections, Charles E. Young Research Library, UCLA.

7. According to Stoller (1997: 71), at the age of twenty-one, Mrs. G was institutionalized at "R State Hospital" after a mental health crisis ("psychotic episode") in which she threatened to kill herself and her children. In R State Hospital she learned she was pregnant with twins. After giving birth she was sterilized. "She says her permission was not asked. Her mother gave permission for the procedure."

8. The citations for this text have publication dates that range from 1967 to 1970, leading me to believe that this report may have been published in the early 1970s.

9. In their book about cross-dressing laws in San Francisco in the nineteenth century, Clare Sears (2015: 75) notes that individuals arrested for cross-dressing often had their case referred to the Insanity Commission, which "returned an insanity verdict in 93 percent of cases."

10. The idea that a mother was to blame for a child's pathology was rampant in both US psychology and popular culture at the time. As Rebecca Jo Plant (2010) writes in her book *Mom: The Transformation of Motherhood in Modern America*, the interwar/

post—World War II era marks a shift from moral motherhood to scientific motherhood, in which the mother's role receded, shifting from an all-encompassing role to the idea of allowing for greater child independence and individuality. During this cultural shift, overbearing mother love began to be seen as narcissistic and pathological. Texts like Philip Wylie's (1942) *Generation of Vipers* argued that mothers were emasculating US society. The rise of antimaternalism coincides with the increasing authority of psychological professionals.

11. Harry Benjamin to Robert Stoller, September 27, 1966, box 25, Harry Benjamin Collection, Kinsey Institute Library and Special Collections, Indiana University, Bloomington.

12. This same kind of mothering was also blamed for homosexuality. At the time of the gender clinics, one of the central pillars of the nascent gay rights movement was the depathologization of homosexuality. Activists would succeed in removing homosexuality from the *Diagnostic and Statistical Manual for Mental Disorders (DSM)* in 1973. Gender identity disorder would be added to the *DSM* in 1980. In this way we can see how the etiological theory of homosexuality pathology was directly carried over to the transsexual. See Milton 2002, Murray 2010.

13. Later in Stoller's career he would pursue this line of inquiry more, travelling to Papua New Guinea in 1979 to study Indigenous populations. In a letter to his colleague Jean-Bertrand Pontalis, he wrote: "I hope to compare their child-rearing techniques and their rituals to measure certain aspects of my theories on the development of masculinity and femininity and erotic behavior." Robert J. Stoller to Jean-Bertrand Pontalis, June 15, 1979, box 32, Robert J. Stoller Papers, Library Special Collections, Charles E. Young Research Library, UCLA.

References

Aizura, Aren Z. 2018. *Mobile Subjects: Transnational Imaginaries of Gender Reassignment*. Durham, NC: Duke University Press.

Benjamin, Harry. 1966. *The Transsexual Phenomenon*. New York: Julian Press.

Freud, Sigmund. 2014. *Three Essays on the Theory of Sexuality*, translated by A. A. Brill. Seaside, OR: Rough Draft Printing.

Gill-Peterson, Jules. 2018. *Histories of the Transgender Child*. Minneapolis: University of Minnesota Press.

Gould, Lois. 1966. "I Ruined My Life When I Changed Sex." *National Insider*, June 12.

Griffin-Gracy, Miss Major. 2017. New York City Trans Oral History Project, December 16. http://oralhistory.nypl.org/interviews/miss-major-griffin-gracy-u29vbz.

Irving, Dan. 2013. "Normalized Transgressions: Legitimizing the Transsexual Body as Productive." In *The Transgender Studies Reader 2*, edited by Susan Stryker and Aren Z. Aizura, 15–29. New York: Routledge.

Milton, Henry L. 2002. *Departing from Deviance: A History of Homosexual Rights and Emancipatory Science in America*. Chicago: University of Chicago Press.

Money, John, and Geoffrey Hosta. 1968. "Negro Folklore of Male Pregnancy." *Journal of Sex Research* 4, no. 1: 34–50.

Moynihan, Daniel Patrick. 1965. "The Negro Family: The Case for National Action." Washington, DC: Office of Policy Planning and Research, United States Department of Labor.

Murray, Heather. 2010. *Not in This Family: Gays and the Meaning of Kinship in Postwar North America*. Philadelphia: University of Pennsylvania Press.

Plant, Rebecca Jo. 2010. *Mom: The Transformation of Motherhood in Modern America*. Chicago: University of Chicago Press.

Sears, Clare. 2015. *Arresting Dress: Cross-Dressing, Law, and Fascination in Nineteenth-Century San Francisco*. Durham, NC: Duke University Press.

Somerville, Siobhan B. 2000. *Queering the Color Line: Race and the Invention of Homosexuality in American Culture*. Durham, NC: Duke University Press.

Spade, Dean. 2006. "Mutilating Gender." In *The Transgender Studies Reader*, edited by Susan Stryker and Stephen Wittle, 315–32. New York: Routledge.

Stern, Alexandra Minna. 2015. "3. Obstetrics and Gynecology." In *University of Michigan: An Encyclopedia Survey*, 32–62. http://hdl.handle.net/2027/spo.13950886.0003.071.

Stoller, Robert J. 1968. *Sex and Gender: On the Development of Masculinity and Femininity*. New York: Science House.

Stoller, Robert J. 1997. *Splitting: A Case of Female Masculinity*. New Haven, CT: Yale University Press.

Weinstein, Deborah. 2013. *The Pathological Family: Postwar America and the Rise of Family Therapy*. Ithaca, NY: Cornell University Press.

Wylie, Philip. 1942. *Generation of Vipers*. New York: Farrar and Rinehart.

TOWARD A BLACK VERNACULAR SEXOLOGY

Aaron J. Stone

*I*n a series of essays published in 1900, Charles Chesnutt—one of the first Black fiction writers to achieve some success on the American literary scene—turned to science to refute racist theories about racial mixing and hypothesize about its results. Chesnutt, who shuttled between running a legal stenography business and trying to make a living writing novels, was by no means a scientist. Yet in "The Future American," Chesnutt ([1900] 2002: 845–46) adopts a tone of scientific authority, reviewing "recent scientific research" to debunk "hoary anthropological fallacies" like the idea that "the shape or size of the head" corresponds to "the civilization or average intelligence of a race." "Proceeding then upon the firm basis laid down by science," Chesnutt propounds his own theory that "the future American race . . . will be formed of a mingling . . . of the various racial varieties" (846–47). He dismisses counterarguments with the air of an exasperated expert, writing that "any theory of sterility due to race crossing . . . is founded mainly on prejudice and cannot be proved by facts" (847). Following quite faithfully the form of a scientific article, Chesnutt here demonstrates his familiarity with racial and sexual science and his eagerness to contribute knowledge to those fields. Chesnutt's foray into scientific discussion exemplifies how turn-of-the-century Black writers felt called to engage scientific theories of race and sexuality that had entered popular discourse and gained authoritative status through high-profile publications. It also suggests how Black literature of the period sought to advance original truth-claims about sexuality, countering an "official" American sexology that excluded Black voices as systematically as it questioned Black humanity.

Benjamin Kahan (2019: 2) argues that sexuality studies has neglected how literary texts contribute to "vernacular sexology," a mode by which "laypeople contest, define, and revise sexual subjectivity in relation to more official modes." Kahan also limits his "claims about sexuality primarily to the white subjects that

GLQ 29:1

DOI 10.1215/10642684-10144378

are the (nearly exclusive) objects of Western sexological case histories" (7), invoking Marlon Ross's (2005) assertion that the history of sexuality has excluded Black subjects because white sexologists subordinated sexual difference to racial difference. Ross rightly critiques the field's reliance on an official, white sexology; when combined with Kahan's (2019: 20) call to consider "modernist literary works as 'vernacular sexology,'" Ross's critique invites us to consider how turn-of-the-century Black literary production made unique contributions to sexological knowledge. What would it mean to excavate a specifically Black vernacular sexology? How does the racialized identity of a Black vernacular sexologist shape the questions, methods, and conclusions of sexual-scientific inquiry? How do Black modes of sexual knowledge production engage with institutional sexology when the latter is often inextricable from scientific racism?

I highlight Black vernacular sexology to emphasize the stakes of this endeavor for turn-of-the-century Black Americans. As Jennifer Terry (1999), Siobhan Somerville (2000), Melissa Stein (2015), and C. Riley Snorton (2017) have respectively shown, sexual and racial sciences have historically amplified cultural anxieties about race and sex, yoked these anxieties together, criminalized Blackness as sexual nonnormativity, and forcibly ungendered Black flesh to facilitate white self-definition. What requires further exploration is how contemporaneous Black subjects presented their own sexological findings. Official turn-of-the-century American sexology consisted of "exploring beliefs, behaviors and bodies, defining the normal and abnormal, and authorizing how and when to intervene" (Reumann 2016: 541). We might define Black vernacular sexology as an unofficial endeavor from a Black standpoint to disseminate knowledge about and perhaps assess particular groups' sexual behaviors, predilections, or values—an endeavor that also often engages institutionalized sexology by deploying, modifying, or refuting its concepts, theories, and methods.

Direct engagements with racialized theories of sexuality appear in Pauline Hopkins's *Contending Forces* (1900), a self-professed romance about a Black woman who overcomes past sexual trauma at the hands of a white man and finds love unexpectedly. Within this marriage plot, the novel makes space for diegetic scientific debates, such as the one that takes place at a meeting of the American Colored League. After a white man defends lynching as justified by the "hellish diabolism" of Black lasciviousness, a Black character named Will Smith counters such theories about his race with experiential knowledge, arguing that the prevalence of Black rape is a fantasy of white bloodthirstiness and that "like the physician sick of a mortal disease, [the Southern white] is unable to prescribe for himself" (Hopkins [1900] 2017: 248, 270). Smith's assertion, that whiteness is the more likely site of dangerous sexual pathology, is reinforced at a dinner frequented by "men deep in scientific research," wherein one Doctor Lewis presents convincing evidence "that [rape] is *not* a characteristic of the black man, although *it is* of the white man of the south" (287, 298; emphasis in original). These diegetic arguments are reinforced by the novel's narrator, who sardonically asserts the superiority of such theories to "any worked out by the most fertile brain of the highly cultured Caucasian" and prescribes "time and moral training among the white men of the South" as "the only cures for concubinage" (87, 332).

Indirect or implicit vernacular engagements with official sexology might take the form of interrogating sexological theories that are integrated into everyday life. Consider, for instance, how Sutton Griggs's novel *The Hindered Hand* (1905) seeks to refute popular theories about Black sexual rapacity reinforced by white supremacist novels like Thomas Dixon's *The Leopard's Spots* (1902), the title of which echoes scientific racism's claims about the biological immutability of Black savagery. In providing counterevidence to such notions, Griggs ([1905] 2017: 5) declares in a preface titled "Solemnly Attested" his commitment to a near-scientific level of truthfulness, averring that "as an intensely absorbed observer" he has composed the novel as "fact . . . in the garb of fiction." In addition to presenting Black sexuality as shy, chaste, and proper, the novel details attempts by white men to entrap Black women into sexual servitude, declaring: "The world at large has heard that the problem of the South is the protection of the white woman. There is another woman in the South" (52).

We might also delimit Black vernacular sexology to observational or experimental modes rather than confessional ones. The genre of the white-life novel, wherein Black authors depict nearly exclusively white characters, uniquely combines the first two modes. Paul Laurence Dunbar's *The Fanatics* (1901), for one, treats white characters as case studies, examining them to make observations about white sexual practices and beliefs. The novel portrays a Civil War–era romance between families of opposite allegiances, positing that certain whites have the perverse privilege of prioritizing sexual attraction over politics. Other abnormalities of white sexual life that Dunbar charts include brazen discussions of sex lives and even performances of erotic intimacy with and around family members and abuses of power by military officers who sexually assault women. Black vernacular sexology need not explicitly state its claims as generalizing—which, when directed toward white subjects, could be dangerous—but some implication of generalizability seems a definitional requirement. Similarly, the examination of "abnormal" sexual predilections, such as we see in Dunbar, is an important hallmark, if not a strict condition, of Black vernacular sexology. In this sense, Black vernacular sexology can expose the contingency of "normality" by presenting normative white sexuality as deviant from a Black perspective.

The above novels are only a few examples of what might be read as Black vernacular sexology. To demonstrate both the importance of and a method for reading Black literary narration as a potential mode of sexological inquiry, I turn in the remainder of this article to an examination of Charles Chesnutt's novel *The Marrow of Tradition* (1901). Published the year after "The Future American," *Marrow* can be read, I propose, against the grain as propounding a vernacular-sexological approach to race and sexuality by training an observational gaze on its white characters. Through a comparative methodology, reading *Marrow* alongside contemporaneous white sexologists, I demonstrate that Chesnutt's novel speaks back to institutional American sexology through a series of reversals, revising theories popularized by the intertwined fields of sexology and race science and refuting the racist claims of these disciplines by scrutinizing white perversion, vice, and criminality. Focusing on the novel's extended case study of a Southern aristocratic ne'er-do-well, I trace *Marrow*'s parodic elaboration of a white male perversion rooted in jealous obsession with Blackness. However, I conclude that, while Chesnutt flirts with the rhetoric of pathologization, he ultimately rejects a minoritizing judgment to propose a broader social theory: that the white supremacist preoccupation with policing the boundaries of the human is truly to blame for the perversion of white individuals. Through this reading, I argue broadly for increased scholarly attention to how Black Americans participated robustly, if unofficially, in the scientific shaping of sex itself.

Chesnutt's fiction emerged onto a late-nineteenth-century literary scene dominated by white supremacist sentiment and racist stereotypes. In Southern local color fiction and nostalgic plantation novels, popular white writers portrayed Blackness as criminal, savage, and not quite human. In response, Chesnutt began his career publishing "frankly propagandistic stories" that "confront the reader with a kind of fictional case study" (Andrews 1980: 81, 76). His fiction fought widely held pseudoscientific beliefs such as those equating racial mixing to biological suicide. In *The Marrow of Tradition*, Chesnutt fictionalizes the 1898 Wilmington Massacre, in which white supremacists in the majority-Black North Carolina city publicly murdered Black citizens to terrorize Black voters and political candidates. Chesnutt's version of this tragedy constitutes *Marrow*'s main plot. A second— and, I argue, sexological—plot follows the white aristocrat Tom Delamere and the Black servant Sandy. Itself a "fictional case study," this plot details Tom's failure to embody masculine ideals and his use of blackface to commit crimes while disguised as Sandy.

Critical readings tend to consider Tom a flat "archetype of the New South," his "lack of masculine character" symbolizing white Southern "degeneration" (Sundquist 1993: 431). Mason Stokes (2001: 109) broke new ground by reading Tom in light of Chesnutt's self-professed familiarity with "various antimasturbatory discourses" and arguing that Tom's criminality and implied onanism replaces "'the Negro as Beast' with 'the white man as Masturbator'" as the primary site of sexual threat. I share Stokes's interest in how Chesnutt represents Tom's perverse sexuality, but my reading differs in a few key ways. First, while Stokes's emphasis on masturbation avoids reading Tom's desires as homosexual, I argue that *Marrow* portrays Tom as exhibiting homoerotic desire toward Sandy. Second, Stokes reads Chesnutt as uncritically deploying regulatory sexual mores, positing that "by demonizing Tom, Chesnutt oddly locates himself within" "the various moralities that make whiteness a successful disciplinary force" (130). I demonstrate that *Marrow*'s examination of Tom tries on the sexologist's judgmental gaze but ultimately critiques it, diagnosing the white propensity to police sexuality as itself a cause of white sexual depravity. Finally, whereas Stokes stops short of calling *Marrow* sexological, I argue that we should read its depiction of Tom as an example of vernacular sexology insofar as the text suggests truth-claims about white sexual behaviors and beliefs while engaging the theories and methods of official sexology.

I demonstrate that *Marrow*'s narrator follows Tom with an exacting gaze as if he were a scientific case study, examining his sexual and moral failings and considering their etiologies. The narration both engages many of the tropes of contemporaneous American sexology and suggests original theories that attend to the racial dynamics of the New South. Instead of diagnosing Tom Delamere as a mere example of New Southern degeneracy, the novel implies that his particular pathology is related to a jealous, erotic obsession with Black masculinity. Moreover, Chesnutt uses the novel's potential for polyvocality to make more complex truth-claims than those that rely on the singular case study. Chesnutt does not let his narrator's deployment of normalizing sexological judgments have the last say; rather, by narrating how the social policing of sexuality contributes to Tom's low self-estimation, Chesnutt ultimately suggests that this very tendency toward sexual policing might be the etiology of white sexual pathology. *Marrow* thus simultaneously deploys sexological methods and theories, revises and subverts them by introducing anti-Black racism as a factor that influences white sexual behavior, and proposes new theories about the etiology of white sexual pathology by attending to how social factors influence individual psychology.

In the novel's first description of Tom, *Marrow*'s narrator assesses him for outward signs of perversion, much as a sexologist would a patient:

> Throwing away the cigarette which he held between his fingers, the young
> man crossed the piazza with a light step. . . .
>
> Slender and of medium height, with a small head of almost per-
> fect contour, a symmetrical face, dark almost to swarthiness, black eyes,
> which moved somewhat restlessly, curly hair of raven tint, a slight mus-
> tache, small hands and feet, and fashionable attire, Tom Delamere . . .
> was easily the handsomest young man in Wellington. But no discriminat-
> ing observer would have characterized his beauty as manly. It conveyed no
> impression of strength, but did possess a certain element, feline rather than
> feminine, which subtly negatived the idea of manliness. (Chesnutt [1901]
> 1993: 15–16)

At first blush, this passage seems more literary than sexological. However, as
Stein (2015: 193) notes: "The belief that character and morality were inscribed
upon the body was so central to nineteenth- and early twentieth-century American cultural and scientific discourse that any feature of a body presupposed to
be deviant could be read as evidence of its abnormality." It is thus most appropriate to read this description as utilizing literary conventions to make observations
consistent with contemporaneous scientific methods. In commenting so extensively
on his physical appearance and the unnamed quality that "subtly negatived the
idea of manliness," the narrator suggests that Tom's gender embodiment belies his
otherwise respectable appearance. Situated as it is from a judgmental perspective, the description press-gangs seemingly innocuous details into signaling an
excess that threatens to unravel Tom's self-assured and handsome exterior. The
cigarette marks him as both carefree and decadent, an early indicator of intemperance and vice. His "light step" is both surefooted and effete. Shapely of head and
symmetrical of face, he possesses no glaring "deformities" that would obviously
imply degeneracy, yet he departs noticeably from the ideals of white masculinity.
Tom's small hands and feet hint at effeminacy, as does his "slender" build and the
implied vanity of his "fashionable attire." Not quite "feminine," there is something
"feline" and animalistically furtive about Tom's appearance.

In this description, Chesnutt uses his narrator to deploy interpretive methods comparable to those of contemporaneous sexological case studies. Remarkably similar is the analysis of physical signs of insufficient masculinity, qualities
that sexologists associated with male sexual perversion. According to William
Lee Howard (1896: 2–3), indicators of the male pervert include intemperance,
unhealthy complexion or comportment, "slight frame," and "effeminate" appearance. G. Frank Lydston (1899: 530) concurs that "male sexual perverts" can be

spotted by their "effeminacy of voice, dress, and manner" and "inferior" physique. Howard's "Realistic but Scientific Account of a True Psychological Case" (1905: 476) contains remarkable similarities to *Marrow*'s description of Tom:

> His figure is slight. . . . His feet are small and his hands delicate. . . . But the man is twenty-eight years old and a theological student. Knowing this you will say, if you are a medical man, that his physical appearance is due to arrested development. There is nothing displeasing about the face or form, except that to the athlete the man would appear as a fit subject for exercise. . . .
>
> His voice is pitched in a low and well-bred tone. . . . It is humanly masculine. . . . Gradually his head drops between his hands, great tremors convulse his delicate frame. . . . Then a great, startlingly great, change comes over the body. A flush appears on his cheeks and the smile of a woman controls his now reddened lips.

As with *Marrow*, Howard's description of this young man presents him as mostly in line with norms of aristocratic masculinity; physical shortcomings like a slight figure, small hands and feet, and lack of athleticism could be chalked up to the "arrested development" of a scholar. Yet both Howard and *Marrow*'s narrator emphasize the latent meaningfulness of these deviations from "humanly masculine" ideals, tethering the not-quite-human to minor deficiencies in manliness. The congruencies between these descriptions illustrate the "revolving door between literature and sexology" (Kahan 2019: 20): *Marrow*'s narrator borrows the sexologist's judgmental gaze just as scientists employed literary techniques to underscore telling details in their case studies. This blurred boundary, yielding in both cases a "realistic but scientific account," further underscores the necessity of attending to Black authors' use of literary description as a discrete intervention into sexological discourse.

The narrator's characterization of Tom as exhibiting "a certain element, feline rather than feminine" (Chesnutt [1901] 1993: 16) also echoes sexologists' insistence that sexual perversion is a vestigial holdover from nonhuman ancestors. James Kiernan (1892: 194) considers sexual perversions "reversions to the ancestral type," drawing a comparison to the "hermaphrodism" of "the lowest animals," an idea that also influenced Lydston's (1889) thinking. R. W. Shufeldt (1907: 21), commenting on the prevalence of homosexuality in humans, marvels that in this aspect humanity "actually out-animals,—yes, out-beasts the bestiality of the very beasts themselves." As such accounts suggest, sexologists viewed "perversion" as an essentially subhuman impulse. By connecting Tom's masculine deficiencies to a "feline" demeanor, *Marrow*'s narrator asserts Tom's perversity, deploying the logic of official sexology to suggest that Tom is not just insufficiently manly, but insufficiently *man*.

The novel further emphasizes how such a dehumanizing characterization is not unlike those wielded against Black Americans. Chesnutt invites this comparison when, a few pages after this description of Tom, he places in the mouth of a white character a similarly animalizing assessment of Sandy, the Black servant to Tom's grandfather. Major Carteret, one of the novel's most virulently white supremacist characters, remarks with reference to Sandy that, while "the negro is capable of a certain doglike fidelity," one must be cautious about Black propensity for theft (Chesnutt [1901] 1993: 24). Carteret's words repeat the ubiquitous claims of race scientists that animality and criminality are inherent to Blackness.[1] By pairing a description of Tom as effetely "feline" with this "doglike" characterization of Sandy, Chesnutt highlights that suspicions of sexual nonnormativity can disqualify whites from full humanity in a way that is isomorphic with, though not identical to, the disqualifications—including perversity—concomitant with what Alexander Weheliye (2014: 4) terms the "racializing assemblages" that constitute Blackness.

Chesnutt here juxtaposes dehumanizing judgments of deviant whiteness with those aimed at demonizing Blackness to examine the phenomenon of jealousy directed from a stigmatized white subject toward an "exemplary" Black one. When Tom's grandfather, John Delamere, objects to the characterization of Sandy as "doglike" by calling him "a gentleman in ebony" (Chesnutt [1901] 1993: 25), the narrator lingers on Tom's discomfort: "Tom could scarcely preserve his gravity at this characterization of old Sandy, with his ridiculous air of importance" (26). Having just highlighted Tom's similarly unstable inhabitation of "manliness," the narrator indicates that this defensive reaction suggests a jealousy on the part of the black sheep toward the Black servant. Through this scene, Chesnutt illustrates the symptoms and causes of white jealousy, connecting Tom's perceived masculine (and human) deficiencies to his envious disdain at Sandy's being lauded as a gentleman.

Marrow further suggests a connection between Tom's envy of Sandy and a desire to imitate him. Hearing about a cakewalk that is to be held at a hotel featuring Black dancers, Tom enters the contest while impersonating Sandy. Wearing blackface makeup and a suit stolen from Sandy, Tom executes his mimicry so precisely that he manages to convince the members of Sandy's church that Sandy himself is performing. While it is tempting to dismiss the impersonation as a whim, *Marrow* signals through the intimacy and precision of Tom's mimicry that there is also something erotic at work. Tom's theft of Sandy's clothes suggests amorous undertones, resonating with Howard's (1896: 5) account of a sexual pervert who "once stole a pair of trousers that she had seen a man wear, and after fondling them had a true venereal orgasm." Moreover, the precision of Tom's impersonation implies extreme intimacy: Tom's imitation of Sandy's "face, his clothes, his voice, his walk" is so exact as to fool several of Sandy's close Black acquaintances beyond any "shadow of doubt" (Chesnutt [1901] 1993: 120). Along with the fact that Tom had only heard about the cakewalk earlier in the evening, this strongly hints that Tom's impersonation is an accomplishment preceded by many hours of diligent observation and practice. *Marrow* thus suggests that Tom, already shown to be jealous of how successfully Sandy performs a gentlemanly role, has long found something instructive in the observation and imitation of his Black rival. In this way, Chesnutt constructs Tom as the ironic inverse of the racist scientific claim that Black Americans can only approach full humanity by becoming "admirable mimics of the whites" (Shufeldt 1907: 108).

Tom's imitation implies both a desire to inhabit Blackness, if only temporarily, and a parallel desire for Sandy that aligns with sexologists' theories about male homosexuality. If Tom, a young man, has been perfecting this imitation for some time, Chesnutt leads us to surmise that Tom has been carefully studying his grandfather's servant since childhood. Lydston (1889: 255) posits that "any powerful impression made upon the sexual system at or near puberty . . . is apt to leave an imprint in the form of sexual peculiarities," and Kiernan (1892: 194) similarly asserts that the male "congenital sexual pervert" develops in his youth a "strong affection to a well-developed man and follows him everywhere." Chesnutt therefore assembles evidence that, by the science of the day, points toward Tom's erotic attraction to and idealization of Sandy's "well-developed" masculinity. The details of this case, however, run counter to the scientific racism upheld by contemporaneous sexology. Combining Tom's mimicry of and envy toward Sandy, Chesnutt implicitly theorizes that white men may develop jealous, even erotic idealizations of Black men in the face of their own perceived deficiencies, diagnosing erotic obsession with Blackness as a specifically white perversion.

Tom's queerness is further evinced by the enumeration of his vices and criminal acts, which institutional sexology linked to sexual perversion. When John Delamere's suspicions of Tom lead him to investigate his grandson's bureau, his police work is amply rewarded: "The contents served to confirm what he had heard concerning his grandson's character. Thrown together in disorderly confusion were bottles of wine and whiskey; soiled packs of cards; a dice-box with dice; a box of poker chips, several revolvers, and a number of photographs and paper-covered books at which the old gentleman merely glanced to ascertain their nature" (Chesnutt [1901] 1993: 222). John's discoveries parody the sexologist's fetishized revelation, uncovering all at once the subject's intertwined sexual and moral failings. Conveniently stashed in one place, these items mirror the logic by which intemperance, avarice, violence, lust, and other vices were viewed by sexologists as interrelated and self-multiplying. Lydston (1889: 254) postulates that a form of "acquired sexual perversion" arises from vice, a theory echoed by Kiernan (1888: 129), who explains that "nerves too frequently irritated by a given stimulus require a new stimulus to rouse them." The bottles in Tom's drawer remind us that many sexologists linked alcoholism to perversion and criminality.[2]

By yoking these vices together, turn-of-the-century sexologists advanced what I call a theory of vicious accretion. As opposed to a unidirectional causal relation, vicious accretion suggests that perversion, vice, and crime all follow from one another interchangeably.[3] The narrator's commentary on Tom reflects this theory: "like most men with one commanding vice, he was addicted to several subsidiary forms of iniquity" (Chesnutt [1901] 1993: 159). With the contents of Tom's bureau literalizing vicious accretion, Chesnutt directs us to read Tom's addiction to vice and crime as simultaneously pointing to sexual perversion. Moreover, by hinting that Tom's perverse preoccupation with Sandy may be the original vice from which others stem, Chesnutt suggests a possibility that white sexologists would not have considered: white perversion may result from an unhealthy obsession with Blackness. As Stokes (2001: 111) points out, Tom's "cryptically described" books and photos must be pornographic, implying that onanism ranks among Tom's vices. Among many others, Kiernan (1888, 1892) argues that masturbation leads to perversion, while Lydston (1899: 527, 557) takes this further, arguing that masturbators can "never become as perfect men," have "no chance at 'normal sexual sensibility,'" and often become criminals.

Playing out sexologists' claims that "crimes, murders especially, are committed through the insane jealousy of homo-sexuals" (Howard 1896: 1), Tom nearly orchestrates Sandy's death. Once again donning his disguise, Tom frames Sandy for the robbery and murder of Tom's aunt. Sandy, thrown in jail and threatened by a lynch mob, seems certain to perish until Tom's scheme is revealed. Carteret, upon discovering Tom's culpability, wonders why Tom commits the crime as Sandy rather than someone unidentifiable: "He would hardly have implicated, out of pure malignity, his grandfather's old servant, who had been his own care-taker for many years" (Chesnutt [1901] 1993: 226). Through Carteret's confusion, Chesnutt implies another, unspeakable explanation: that a jealous sexual passion might have justified Tom's attempt to frame Sandy and murder his darling by proxy.

Against official sexology's reinforcement of white supremacy, Chesnutt raises the possibility that "jealousy of the negro's progress" is itself culpable for perceived linkages among perversion, vice, and crime (238).

Through Tom's framing of Sandy, Chesnutt explicitly refutes scientific racism's insistence on Black criminality, illustrating how crimes committed by whites are routinely pinned on innocent Black citizens. *Marrow*'s narrator details the faulty science by which white supremacy seizes on crime to terrorize Black Americans: "It must not be imagined that any logic was needed, or any reasoning consciously worked out. The mere suggestion that the crime had been committed by a negro was equivalent to proof against any negro" (179). Through Carteret, Chesnutt disapprovingly reiterates white sexologists' belief that Black crime often had sexual motivations stemming from inherent savagery: "Left to his own degraded ancestral instincts, Sandy had begun to deteriorate. . . . The criminal was a negro, the victim a white woman;—it was only reasonable to expect the worst" (182).[4] Carteret echoes Howard's (1904: 905–6) assertion that Black "attacks on defenseless white women are evidences of racial instincts" that are not "amenable to ethical culture." Shufeldt (1907: 120) even claims that "eighty-five per cent. of the crimes committed in the Southern States are committed by negroes." *Marrow*'s narrator seems to respond directly to such statements, describing how "statistics of crime" are "ingeniously manipulated" to support racist beliefs (Chesnutt [1901] 1993: 238). Tom's incognito offenses reverse the presumption of Black criminality, parodying the extent to which all crime is attributed to an always already perverse Blackness and theorizing instead the essential whiteness of criminality.

In writing Tom, Chesnutt has his cake(walk) and eats it too. Adopting a "rational," scientific gaze, *Marrow*'s narrator does to Tom what sexologists do to queer and Black subjects: he renders Tom an overdetermined symbol of everything vicious. Chesnutt as author thus indirectly deploys a Black scientific gaze through his narrator to diagnose perversity in a white subject. However, this analysis is not merely a vengeful pathologization of a white individual. The narrator's scrutiny of Tom ironically employs the language of individual pathology to allow Chesnutt to critique the deeper social dysfunction inherent in scientific calls for disciplinary policing. *Marrow* implies that, even if Tom is the degenerate he seems to be, the theory of vicious accretion has enacted itself as a self-fulfilling prophecy. Whereas race scientists claimed that there was something inherently perverse about Black and queer subjects, Chesnutt's depiction of Tom's descent into vice ultimately critiques the panoptic policing of Southern white masculinity.

Marrow points to disciplinary power in its first description of Tom. When the narrator states that "no discriminating observer would have characterized his beauty as manly," he voices the sexologist's belief that a trained eye can see through deceptive surfaces to locate perversion even in ostensibly respectable individuals (16). Howard (1896: 3) even posits that certain sexual perversions manifest as a "lycanthropic condition" that can induce in even a respectable-seeming man such a craving for semen that "he would not stop at murder to obtain his quantum of this disgusting stimulant." Lydston (1899: 530) further writes that, while external signs can help one spot sexual perverts, "exceptions to this rule are numerous." Enumerating these signs and their exceptions ensured that sexologists could stoke fears about hidden perversions while asserting that only careful, knowing observation could be trusted to identify deviants.

Marrow's "discriminating observer," however, is not a literal sexologist but a vigilant layperson, indicating the widespread belief that special scientific knowledge is not necessarily required to suss out deviance. "Discriminating" here simultaneously signifies privileged scientific skills and the above-average perceptivity of a cultured layperson. The effect is both to raise the layperson's biased suspicions to the heightened plane of scientific knowledge and to lower the scientist's claims of authority to a position on par with general wisdom. The "discriminating observer" thus parodies sexologists' and race scientists' appeals to common sense, ironizing their reliance on nonscientific truth-claims and pointing out their incitements of disciplinary regulation. Such appeals abound in Shufeldt's (1907: 116) writing: "Negroes . . . menace all that is decent in a developing nation. . . . Ask any intelligent Southern man or woman and he or she will tell you something of the state of affairs there existing, even if such people do not grasp the danger in its fullness as the far-seeing and philosophic biologist and anthropologist does." Such a belief, Shufeldt declares, is unassailable because of its prevalence among "intelligent" (white) Southerners, although he is quick to assert defensively that the scientist's insights are not merely affirmative recapitulations of public sentiment. These appeals allow Shufeldt to make sweeping generalizations about Black Americans without the burden of evidence: "Every one who knows anything of the typical negro, knows full well that he is an utterly non-moral being" (130). Racist beliefs, no matter how indefensible, might thus be shrouded in the authority of the scientist.

Because these powers of discrimination were posited as within the grasp of any "intelligent" person, sexologists and race scientists incited laypeople to police one another for signs of perversion, vice, and criminality. By exposing this practice, Chesnutt makes a claim that white sexologists do not: the policing of full humanity, combined with the theory of vicious accretion, actually contributes to vice and crime by demonizing suspected perverts as already not quite human and pushing them to jealousy and desperation. *Marrow* suggests that constant surveillance has caused Tom to judge himself as deviant and to view his own "perversions" as self-multiplying. Lee Ellis, Tom's rival, is depicted as incessantly on guard for evidence of Tom's misdeeds. It is reported that "Ellis saw Delamere with the eye of a jealous rival, and judged him mercilessly,—whether correctly or not the sequel will show" (Chesnutt [1901] 1993, 19). With this final phrase, attention is drawn to the fact that, poor though Tom's character may be, Ellis's morbid preoccupation with proving Tom's deficiency may itself drive Tom further into vice. It is further remarked that "Ellis had been watching Delamere for a year," which led him to "note things about his favored rival which might have escaped the attention of others less concerned" (95). Ellis's judgments of Tom render him a white sexologist in his own right—we can only guess whether his nominal relation to Havelock Ellis is coincidental—allowing Chesnutt to critique the incitements to policing inherent in scientists' theories: "To Ellis . . . biased perhaps by jealousy, Tom Delamere was a type of the degenerate aristocrat. If, as he had often heard, it took three or four generations to make a gentleman, and as many more to complete the curve and return to the base . . . Tom Delamere belonged somewhere on the downward slant, with large possibilities of further decline" (95–96). Ellis's having "often heard" such theories accounts for the prevalence of sexological ideas among white Americans, and his application of those theories to his interpretation and policing of Tom illustrates the extent to which official sexology encouraged surveillant amateur versions. This underscoring of Ellis's jealousy further implies that disciplinarity encourages those deemed phenotypically white to compete for proper whiteness or drift toward the not quite human.

    Marrow describes such surveillance as well known to Tom, indicating the potential for surveillance to engender the deviance it seeks. When rumors about Tom's propensities for gambling and drinking make their way to Carteret, Carteret warns Tom about these vices, "disturb[ing] slightly [Tom's] sense of security" and rather "disquiet[ing] him," leading Tom to paranoia (94). While Chesnutt could not be accused of portraying Tom in a sympathetic light, his examination of sexual policing refutes the standard sexological claim that criminality such as Tom's is linked to innate masculine and sexual deficiencies. Rather, Chesnutt posits that Tom's behavior is the product of a disciplinary apparatus that constructs Tom—to himself as well as others—as irreparably deficient from the outset. *Marrow* thus implies that Tom's perverse attraction to and desire to embody a fetishized Blackness stem from the urge to escape the tightly policed boundaries of whiteness. When the stigma of deviance threatens one's access to full humanity, Chesnutt postulates, subjects deemed deficient often divest from the social order entirely.

It is by this mechanism, *Marrow* implies, that white supremacy cannibalizes even its own. This is the payoff of Chesnutt's sexological reversals: against scientists' dehumanizing assertions of Black savagery, the novel argues that true inhumanity undergirds white disciplinary power. Chesnutt's identification of white savagery is, of course, most obvious in the examples of vigilante acts of white juridical power, such as lynchings and massacres, that he also depicts. But in his examination of the impacts of sexological theories, Chesnutt adds a less obvious diagnosis: that imposture, precarity, and jealousy form the perverse center of white supremacy. Such insights demonstrate the importance of attending to Black vernacular sexology in the form of literary texts so as to uncover further how Black voices have refined and refused hegemonic theories of sex itself.

Notes

1. See, e.g., Howard 1904; Kiernan 1888; Lydston 1899, l904; McGuire and Lydston 1893; Rosse 1892; Shufeldt 1891, 1907.
2. See, e.g., Howard 1896; Hughes 1893; Lydston 1889, 1912; Lydston and Talbot 1891.
3. See also Kahan's (2019: 100–114) account of "volitional etiologies" and Michel Foucault's (2003: 282) notion of "decompartmentalization," on which Kahan elaborates.
4. Kiernan and Lydston each claim that Black men are susceptible to attacks of *furor sexualis* during which obsession with fulfilling a sexual aim leads to crime, assault, and violence. See Kiernan 1885; Lydston 1896, 1899; McGuire and Lydston 1893.

References

Andrews, William L. 1980. *The Literary Career of Charles W. Chesnutt*. Baton Rouge: Louisiana State University Press.

Chesnutt, Charles W. (1900) 2002. "The Future American." In *Charles W. Chesnutt: Stories, Novels, and Essays*, edited by Werner Sollors, 845–63. New York: Library of America.

Chesnutt, Charles W. (1901) 1993. *The Marrow of Tradition*. New York: Penguin.

Dunbar, Paul Laurence. (1901) 1969. *The Fanatics*. New York: Negro Universities Press.

Foucault, Michel. 2003. *Abnormal: Lectures at the Collège de France, 1974–1975*. London: Verso.

Griggs, Sutton E. (1905) 2017. *The Hindered Hand; or, The Reign of the Repressionist*, edited by John Cullen Gruesser and Hanna Wallinger. Morgantown: West Virginia University Press.

Hopkins, Pauline E. (1900) 1988. *Contending Forces: A Romance Illustrative of Negro Life North and South*. Oxford: Oxford University Press.

Howard, William Lee. 1896. "Sexual Perversion." *Alienist and Neurologist* 17, no. 1: 1–6.

Howard, William Lee. 1904. "The Negro as a Distinct Ethnic Factor." *Medical News* 84, no. 19: 905–6.

Howard, William Lee. 1905. "Two Souls in One Body: A Realistic but Scientific Account of a True Psychological Case." *The Arena* 34, no. 192: 476–79.

Hughes, Charles H. 1893. "Erotopathia—Morbid Erotism." *Alienist and Neurologist* 14, no. 4: 531–78.

Kahan, Benjamin. 2019. *The Book of Minor Perverts: Sexology, Etiology, and the Emergences of Sexuality*. Chicago: University of Chicago Press.

Kiernan, James G. 1885. "Race and Insanity: The Negro Race." *Journal of Nervous and Mental Disease* 12, no. 3: 290–93.

Kiernan, James G. 1888. "Sexual Perversion and the Whitechapel Murders." *Medical Standard* 4, no. 6: 129–30, 170–72.

Kiernan, James G. 1892. "Responsibility in Sexual Perversion." *Chicago Medical Recorder* 3, no. 3: 185–210.

Lydston, G. Frank. 1889. "Clinical Lecture: Sexual Perversion, Satyriasis and Nymphomania." *Philadelphia Medical and Surgical Reporter* 61, no. 10: 253–58, 281–85.

Lydston, G. Frank. 1896. "Asexualization in the Prevention of Crime." *Medical News* 68, no. 21: 573–78.

Lydston, G. Frank. 1899. *The Surgical Diseases of the Genito-Urinary Tract: Venereal and Sexual Diseases*. Philadelphia, PA: F. A. Davis.

Lydston, G. Frank. 1904. *The Diseases of Society: The Vice and Crime Problem*. Philadelphia, PA: J. B. Lippincott.

Lydston, G. Frank. 1912. "Sex Mutilations in Social Therapeutics: With Some of the Difficulties in the Way of the Practical Application of Eugenics to the Human Race." *New York Medical Journal* 95, no. 14: 677–85.

Lydston, G. Frank, and E. S. Talbot. 1891. "Studies of Criminals: Degeneracy of Cranial and Maxillary Development in the Criminal Class, with a Series of Illustrations of Criminal Skulls and Histories Typical of the Physical Degeneracy of the Criminal Deformities of the Jaw as Seen in Criminals." *Alienist and Neurologist* 12, no. 4: 556–85.

McGuire, Hunter, and G. Frank Lydston. 1893. *Sexual Crimes among the Southern Negroes*. Louisville, KY: Renz and Henry.

Reumann, Miriam G. 2016. "Sex and Science." In *A Companion to the History of American Science*, edited by Georgina M. Montgomery and Mark A. Largent, 541–52. Oxford: Wiley.

Ross, Marlon. 2005. "Beyond the Closet as Raceless Paradigm." In *Black Queer Studies: A Critical Anthology*, edited by E. Patrick Johnson and Mae G. Henderson, 161–89. Durham, NC: Duke University Press.

Rosse, Irving C. 1892. "Sexual Hypochondriasis and Perversion of the Genesic Instinct." *Journal of Nervous and Mental Disease* 17, no. 11: 795–811.

Shufeldt, R. W. 1891. "Crime among Washington Negroes." *Science* 18, no. 445: 94–95.

Shufeldt, R. W. 1907. *The Negro: A Menace to American Civilization*. Boston: R. G. Badger.

Snorton, C. Riley. 2017. *Black on Both Sides: A Racial History of Trans Identity*. Minneapolis: University of Minnesota Press.

Somerville, Siobhan B. 2000. *Queering the Color Line: Race and the Invention of Homosexuality in American Culture*. Durham, NC: Duke University Press.

Stein, Melissa N. 2015. *Measuring Manhood: Race and the Science of Masculinity, 1830–1934*. Minneapolis: University of Minnesota Press.

Stokes, Mason. 2001. *The Color of Sex: Whiteness, Heterosexuality, and the Fictions of White Supremacy*. Durham, NC: Duke University Press.

Sundquist, Eric J. 1993. *To Wake the Nations: Race in the Making of American Literature*. Cambridge, MA: Harvard University Press.

Terry, Jennifer. 1999. *An American Obsession: Science, Medicine, and Homosexuality in Modern Society*. Chicago: University of Chicago Press.

Weheliye, Alexander. 2014. *Habeas Viscus: Racializing Assemblages, Biopolitics, and Black Feminist Theories of the Human*. Durham, NC: Duke University Press.

THE ANATOMY OF HABIT

Prison Sexology and the Scandal of Pederasty in Colonial India

Rovel Sequeira

*T*estifying before the Indian Jails Committee in 1919, Irish medical officer John Mulvany stunned the colonial administration by accusing Walter Buchanan, a current member of the committee and the outgoing inspector-general of Bengal prisons, of burying his research on sodomy or pederasty in Indian jails.[1] In 1905, on commencing his medical-scientific studies at Calcutta's Presidency Jail, Mulvany was warned that "it was a subject about which the Government desired to know nothing" (*Indian Jails Committee* 1921: 2:40). Since Mulvany's "investigations had made him extremely unpopular in jail and his life had been attempted more than once," he seemingly desisted, while secretly beginning new "experiments" at the nearby Alipore New Central Jail in 1913 (40). By 1919, he exposed the scandal within the colonial bureaucracy, citing numerous intercepted love letters between prisoners as exemplary evidence of prison pederasty's ubiquity.

Excavating the contours of this previously unstudied scandal, I examine the early twentieth-century Indian prison as a colonial sexological laboratory, arguing that it grounded a spatial form of sexual science tied to the science of confinement. I will show, first, that Mulvany's experiments on subaltern sexual "deviants" developed in tandem with and helped reconstitute the architecture of the prisons he administered. Instrumentalizing racialized criminological theories about Indian prisoners' affinity for sociability over privacy, he isolated sex offenders in cellular confinement instead of in standard association wards to correct their deviance. Second, I explore how Mulvany's investigations shifted from foregrounding anatomical observation to intercepting the intimate letters of sequestered prisoners, a practice that I argue paradoxically led him to negate their individuality rather than attend to it. That is, although the vocal evidence of enduring same-sex affinities

GLQ 29:1
DOI 10.1215/10642684-10144392
© 2023 by Duke University Press

in the letters might have allowed him to localize sodomy as the interiorized truth of the prisoner's self, it instead helped shift the imagination of Indian "unnatural vice" from repeated criminality to a racialized collective notion of habitual excess. Finally, I will document how the state prevented the circulation of Mulvany's evidence, anticipating outcry about having exposed Indian political prisoners to sexual abuse. By coding Mulvany's studies as unscientific and preventing them from producing a public scandal, the state maintained the incarceration of prisoners in overcrowded jails. While scholars have predominantly studied the circulation of sexology among imperial bourgeois publics, I theorize how the state's dominance over penology amplifies our understanding of subaltern Indian sexual life and of the infrastructural nodes subtending sexology. In doing so, I "provincialize" European sexological histories, showing how colonial investments in maintaining selective ignorance about prison sexual life rather than merely producing knowledge about it enabled both disciplinary and repressive exercises of power.

Perverse Modernity: Prisoner Classification
and the Taxonomy of Jail Space

Before discussing Mulvany's experiments, it is instructive to consider the specific colonial penal history they interrupted. As David Arnold (1992: 28) has shown, colonial biomedicine was centralized through bounded spatial grids like jails, hospitals, and army barracks until the late nineteenth century; prisoners doubled as labor for infrastructural projects as well as expedient subjects for biomedical research on mortality. Confinement, not reform, was the nineteenth-century goal of imprisonment, so that while "the body of the 'Oriental' might be disciplined, his 'soul' remained out of reach" (175). Reform was periodically advocated by jail administrators (rather than those on the margins of the state), but limited finances and perceived differences in Indian criminality were used to justify punishments like flogging well into the twentieth century (161). When the state initiated the 1919 Jails Committee for an overhaul, however, it faced a growing nationalist movement and had conceded some future control over provincial jails to Indians. Consequently, the committee was forced to admit that penology had "failed so far to regard the prisoner as an individual rather [than] a unit in the jail" (*Indian Jails Committee* 1921: 1:31).

The prison system in early twentieth-century India comprised a patchwork of buildings built to different plans, most containing association wards for twenty to fifty prisoners, with cells for smaller numbers (Waits 2018). While many argued that this system's failure (whether in separating adults from juveniles, or in segre-

gating first-time offenders from hardened criminals) stemmed from the lack of cellular jails on the British model, cellular confinement itself was "losing ground" as
a reformative theory, as modern US prisons showed (*Indian Jails Committee* 1921:
1:101). When Indian jails were occasionally constructed on cellular lines, they
soon fell into disuse due to concerns of climate, sanitation, or capacity (Sen 2000).
Unlike Europeans, moreover, Indians were perceived as "sociable and averse to
solitude" by "custom and habit" (*Indian Jails Committee* 1921, 1:31). Indeed,
committee officials argued that Indian prisoners were well primed to return to
society *because* of the association system. Rather than individualizing the prisoner,
cellular confinement contradicted the modern "treatment of prisoners as individuals and not as a herd" because it merely placed "each individual in an individual
cell" in a one-size-fits-all solution (101). How then should we read the intermittent
onset of cellular confinement in India, if not as the belated arrival of modernity?

When committee members did recommend cellular incarceration, they perceived it as harsher than confinement in association, not as a solution that would
remediate prisoners' souls. Cellular confinement would automatically achieve the
desired separation of adults from juveniles and habitual from casual or first-time
offenders while preventing any transmission of criminal "habits." Consequently,
the committee reached consensus in retaining association for first-timers and cellular incarceration for "habituals," seemingly seeking individualization for all
according to their criminal antecedents. But in doing so, it came perilously close
to implying that India's association-based system was already modern and had
evolved to address the specificities of Indian criminality.

Because one could only be assigned to confinement after close scrutiny,
prison officials systematically classified incarcerated people as either habitual or
casual offenders, a process that now assumed renewed priority. The nineteenth-
century colonial discourse of habitual criminality itself derived from the racialized
and spatialized taxonomy of Indian "criminal tribes" (Yang 1985). The habitual
criminal was perceived as an urban figure who had become accustomed to crime,
in contrast with the hereditary criminal, who had been linked with intergenera-
tional rural or "tribal" crime (Sen 2000). That these typologies overlapped, however, was clarified in 1886, when habit was procedurally defined as recidivism to
account for both: any repeated offense against property and a minimal previous
sentence of three years' imprisonment would merit the classification of "habitual."
But such classification conflated "varying degrees of criminality" from petty theft
to armed dacoity without presuming any necessary "moral corruption" of the criminal (*Indian Jails Committee* 1921: 1:75–76). To stretch the category to account
for so-called criminal morality, the committee urged the medical administrator

to discern whether prisoners had developed a criminal habit *in prison* or *out of prison* along with considering his prior convictions. As significantly, they recommended adding repeat offenses against persons—like murder, rape, and *unnatural vice/crime*—to the definition of "habit." "Unnatural vice" became the limit case in this definition because individuals rarely entered prison for the crime of sodomy; rather, as the committee noted, prison itself "addicted [the criminal] to the practice" (81). Consequently, the figure of the habitual sodomite or pederast was rendered constitutive of the discursive grammar of penology, as I will elaborate through Mulvany's experiments.[2]

Criminal Habits: Anatomy and the Speculative Science of Pederasty

Charged with reducing jail mortality in the 1860s, civil surgeons of the Indian Medical Service (IMS) doubled as prison superintendents. Entering the IMS in the fin de siècle, Mulvany began overseeing Calcutta's Presidency Jail in 1902. Among the oldest colonial jails, Presidency was an eighteenth-century structure that served as a halfway house for transporting prisoners to the Andaman Islands penal settlement. Since "functional specificity was largely absent from its design," it was retrofitted with iron-wired cubicles in the mid-nineteenth century, but it was still considered flawed because prisoners could not be adequately separated, despite such architectural improvisations (Waits 2018: 154–55).

After assuming charge, Mulvany noticed that prisoners commonly left their beds at night to visit other prisoners. Upon conducting medical exams of the same people, he discovered that their bodies "presented in a marked degree the distinctive anatomical signs characteristic of the passive agent in sodomy" (Mulvany 1921a: 412).[3] He also began to suspect that prisoners applied for convict-officer posts due to the "facility [of committing] unnatural offences" (412). On anatomically examining each applicant, he found it difficult to discover "active" sodomy but disqualified the "passive habitués of this vice" from overseer roles (413). Moreover, he elaborated a probabilistic schematic for sodomy, estimating that 30 percent of all prisoners were "active" sodomites, and 50 percent were "passive" catamites (413). As the average Presidency population was 1,100, an astronomically high 800 were logically "sodomites or catamites or both" (413). But even separating known "catamites" at night could not prevent infractions; in one instance, prisoners were found having sex "midday" in a crowded ward, leading Mulvany to conclude that they were "lost to that sense of shame, which ordinarily relegates such offences to solitude" (413). Placing pederasty on a continuum of early and supposedly excessive Indian exposure to sexuality from child marriage onward, he argued that the "oriental, accustomed from the most tender ages, to free exercise of the sexual functions," treated "unnatural vice" merely like "female prostitution"; this accounted for pederasty's prevalence in India to a "hardly conceivable" degree, only paralleled by ancient Greece (412–13).

From the data he derived from corporeal examinations, Mulvany theorized that novice delinquents became hardened criminals *because of* incarceration. For him, "in oriental countries, the social disgrace" of imprisonment was "less than among western nations" and the prisoner's jail life blunted this residual shame (411). "Rarely a family man," the would-be habitual forgot domestic life in prison because governmental policy was to displace prisoners from their local "criminal" networks by placing them in far-flung jails (411). Consequently, the prisoner found himself adrift: "family ties are severed" and the criminal, "relieved from" earning his keep, began treating prison as his "father-in-law's house" (413). In prison, unpaid convict-officers facilitated a roaring trade in ganja, opium, and tobacco. As Mulvany forcefully contended, the easiest way for convicts to obtain such contraband was "paiderasty"; prisoners' tendency to commodify their bodies in exchange for such goods (and presumably, also for pleasure) made prison sex among "the most potent factors" for recidivism (412).

Clearly, Mulvany's physiological examinations generated incomplete evidence, which, in turn, led him to conjecture sodomy's monumental scale. He instrumentalized prisoners' bodies through a politics of surmise in which "rather than acknowledge conjecture as conjecture, surmise stakes an ontological claim" as uncontestable fact (Weston 2008: 223). Such evidentiary lack authorized ongoing dehumanizing probes of prisoners' bodies and further repression. For instance, it allowed Mulvany to advocate a punitive labor regime for "habitual sodomites," to urge their—and ideally, every prisoner's—confinement in cells, and to recommend abolishing the convict-officer system altogether (Mulvany 1921a: 413). Only then would forced sexual abstinence be "one of the greatest [penal] privations," voiding jail of "charms" that might otherwise incite prisoners to further crime (413).

Like his contemporaries, Mulvany understood sodomy/pederasty through a narrow rhetorical register of "unnatural" offenses, codified in the 1860s through section 377 of the Indian Penal Code. Though stilted, this vocabulary eloquently coded same-sex sexual acts, irrespective of age, as "unspeakable" until the 1920s (accounting for why Mulvany used the terms interchangeably) (Puri 2017). In contrast, an elaborate vocabulary described prisoners themselves, based on their infractions outside (and conduct inside) prison: from political prisoners to A-class prisoners (first-time offenders) to B- and C-class "habituals." Thus categorized, prisoners were to wear distinct bodily accessories, from clothing to restraints, which rendered them hypervisible and reinforced hierarchized sociability within prison (Anderson 2004). Consider, for instance, Mulvany's recommendation that sex offenders be categorized as C-class habituals, separate from B-class prisoners incarcerated for offenses against property. In Bengal, the latter already wore black caps to prevent their interaction with first-timers. On Mulvany's orders, the neck-tickets of "recognized catamites" at Presidency, worn on iron neck rings, had holes punched into them. But tailored neck-tickets began to stamp "the immoral character of the individual" on his body, presumably making it easier to approach him for sex, so Mulvany began marking sexual offenses in prisoners' "history sheets" instead (Mulvany 1921a: 412). Similar problems arose in disciplining prisoners' bodies through sumptuary regulations. In the Andaman Islands, administrators assigned "catamites" to the habitual recipient labor gang, identified by chocolate-striped uniforms (Anderson 2004: 119). But since this attire drew "the attention of all," the practice ceased in 1906; henceforth, they were incarcerated in cells "specially set apart," like other "habitual" prisoners (*Report on the Administration* 1908: 16).

Unsurprisingly, then, the committee held that though the "sodomite" was not "ordinarily held to fall within the present definition of a habitual criminal," he had to be "isolated, on moral grounds" (*Indian Jails Committee* 1921: 1:81). Habit continued to be defined procedurally as a repeated offense, but the committee implicitly sanctioned individual penologists and doctors to ascertain the criminal's disposition to habitual sodomy within prison. As Kath Weston (2008: 224) has astutely observed, the habitual sex offender "occupied that middle ground where acts and identities, behavior and species-being, enjoyed greater intimacy than many theorists have allowed."

Inmates in Love: Prisoners' Voices and the Evidentiary Protocols of Prison Sexology

As his Presidency record makes explicit, Mulvany sought to reorder the gradations of jail space through the sodomite's body—and vice versa. On taking charge of the newly built New Central Jail in Alipore in 1913, he isolated sex offenders in experimental forms of confinement unavailable at Presidency. He designed the jail himself on British lines, following the 1870s radial plan of Bhagalpore Central Jail. Here, he developed a byzantine system of segregation—solitary, cellular, and separate—to limit prisoners' ability to see and talk to others and to prevent sexual encounters between them. These gradations were influenced by his tour inspecting metropolitan British penological trends in 1910. Departing from his earlier preferences, he now argued that "to shut up human beings in separate cells for 13 to 14 hours every day is simply ruination to the individual, body and soul" (*Indian Jails Committee* 1921: 2:52).

Mulvany's newfound opposition to blanket seclusion derived also from colonial experiments in confining political prisoners; in his own words, he "had more to do with the imprisonment of political prisoners than any jail officer in India" (*Indian Jails Committee* 1921: 2:37). For instance, he was ordered to inflict six months' isolation on members of Bengal's revolutionary terrorist movement in the early 1910s. Complaining to Buchanan, his superior, he argued that such confinement would "drive a sensitive man insane" (37). Mulvany observed that when prisoners were indefinitely quarantined, they were initially anxious for release but eventually became apathetic or insensate. His interrogators questioned this conclusion, suggesting that such mental deterioration in confinement was a "racial peculiarity" of "sedentary" Bengalis, rather than of "the Pathan, Baluchi, or Mahratta" (76). Clearly deriving from the nineteenth-century "martial races" stereotype of Bengali effeminacy, this racial discourse contravened Mulvany's experience with even his non-Bengali prisoners (Sinha 1995). Though his superiors even questioned "what introspection an ordinary *ryot* [Hindu peasant] put in for 7 days in a solitary cell is likely to go through," he countered their racial and class biases and advocated shortened isolation as both deterrent and reformatory for preventing specific offenses, allowing prisoners to reflect on their infractions without subjecting them to lasting psychological harm (Indian Jails Committee 1921: 2:77). In the case of the revolutionaries, however, Buchanan induced him to withdraw his protest and submit a misleadingly sanguine report about their health; doing otherwise would rouse the state's "Olympian wrath" (Mulvany 1921b: 414).

Mulvany's experiments on sex offenders also shifted to align with his new psychological theories. In his 1898 *Manual on Jail Hygiene*, Buchanan had reluctantly broached the sex life of "lunatic" prisoners, following the biomedical belief that sodomy was a symptom of insanity. By 1919, however, Mulvany regularly cited Havelock Ellis's penological work (and occasionally, his foundational psychiatric idioms of "sexual inversion" for sodomy), demonstrating his growing engagement with global penological and sexological trends. But since prison officers were recruited from the European-dominated IMS, they lacked specialized knowledge not only of psychiatry but also of local customs and languages. Undoubtedly, this racial and linguistic gulf precluded full recognition of prisoners' own sexual cosmologies. Despite Mulvany's interest in the individualizing vocabularies of imperial-metropolitan penology (and sexology), he too sought to understand sodomy from the standpoint of (dis)order rather than identity. Contrary to Michel Foucault's (1978) stress on "sexuality" as an individualizing disciplin-

ary technology in Europe, I argue, therefore, that colonial prison sexology habitu-
ally reduced prisoners to their anatomies—bodies to be corrected, not selves to
be rehabilitated—even while ostensibly seeking to individualize the treatment of
their psyches.

Consider Mulvany's second "experiment" on sex offenders at Alipore, involving the interception of their love letters. Prisoners were then only allowed one letter
every four to six months, often dictated to a designated convict writer. Inmates were
denied writing materials because they could use them to pass subversive messages
or escape plans, and every letter was translated and censored by the prison inter-
preter. Unlike ordinary correspondence, the missives Mulvany seized were probably penned on stolen paper and delivered by bribed overseers. Additionally, many
Alipore prisoners worked for the adjoining Government Press, suggesting that some
might have been neoliterate. Consequently, I suggest that the letters' skeletal structure and clipped rhythms index the pressures under which they were written. At
times, they also illustrate the categories through which their authors were appre-
hended by prison sexology and came to (mis)recognize themselves.

By way of illustration, consider the two letters below:

HIRA LAL,

You may take food from anyone you like. But if you don't take food
from me, I will stop speaking to you. I take you as my brother, I fed you for
three months and I shall be able to feed you for 3 months more. . . . No one
will dare to touch you as long as I am there.

[16699 B-4, Nagendra Nath Das, 22 years, 6 M. under 380–75
I.P.C.]

GONESH

I have not received the 4 anna bit which was taken by Mongla. If we
quarrel we will both be placed in cells. What do you advise? Let me have
a reply. He has slapped me. What do you wish me to do? . . . If I am placed
in cells, we will not meet.

[Unsigned][4]

Such letters convey little about the sender or receiver. Only the truncated colonial
categories supplied by a prison administrator provide the contents of the writers'
"life history." For instance, we can tell that Das was a B-class "habitual" and that
he was twenty-two years old when reconvicted of house-burgling and sentenced
to six months' imprisonment. Evidently, he also provided food and protection to

Hira Lal in prison, considering him his beloved "brother." From the similarly terse latter note, it appears that Gonesh was the writer's "patron" and sent him money, probably through an overseer. This message was clearly also written under constraint—the letter is unsigned, perhaps to prevent detection; the go-between appropriated the writer's funds and assaulted him; and Gonesh feared further confinement.

The following letters are barely more communicative:

DEAREST LATIF,

Received your letter yesterday and came to know everything. From this day you cannot expect anything from me. I have not been giving you Rs. 5 or 7 monthly for so long so that you might become the chokra of Gaffur [a notorious black-cap]. However, if you wish to be my chokra, come today anyhow, nitting [*sic*] Kala topi [a black cap] through Nos. 10 and 11 wards. . . .

(Sd.) NILKANTO

[14208 B-2, 27 years, July 1917]

You SALA MUSALA,

Had your father ever any chokra? You are a beggar. You, Sala fed Pancha and made a friendship with him. Everyone should keep one man only. Pancha doesn't want anything from you. . . .

[16025 B-13, Shaikh Yasin, 13 years, December 1917]

As the *Hobson-Jobson* dictionary of Anglo-Indian creole notes, the Hindustani word *chokra* denoted a boy/youngster "employed about the household, or a regiment."[5] Signifying servitude, the term *chokra* apparently entered prisoners' vocabularies to indicate a beloved or dependent (sexually and materially). For Mulvany, *chokras* lacked agency and were invariably corrupted by older men. But such hierarchies were not predicated solely upon age, despite Mulvany's claim that "nine-tenths of the crime is committed by immature boys who are led astray by these incorrigibles" (*Indian Jails Committee* 1921, 2:60). Clearly, the writer of the letter above, a thirteen-year-old, felt comfortable threatening a fellow Muslim inmate over the right to support his own *chokra* (who could hardly be much younger).

Undoubtedly, prison erotic relations did have to navigate hierarchies of religion, caste, and age, but they were less determined by such differences than by hierarchies between experienced prisoners and newcomers. At times, such relations could turn violent:

Look here LALOO,

> Save us. Don't admit anything. If you confess then both you and we shall suffer. . . . Tell what I advise you, or else I shall cut you when I get out. . . . You are a mere boy. . . . No grave intimacy should be made in jail. People speak ill. . . .
> [To Undertrial prisoner, July 1918]

Here, Laloo appears to have committed an unspecified crime with some men but was not tried with them due to his youth. Housed in the same prison while awaiting his sentence, he was both threatened and educated by others in the codes of "civility" and survival in prison.

Targeting the effects of such insufficient segregation, Mulvany attacked the overcrowding of jails and the subsequent difficulty of classifying and separating prisoners of different ages. For him, this "failure" added to "the nocturnal orgies of vice [in] our Indian jails, [providing] a perennial supply of recruits to the great army of recidivism" (*Indian Jails Committee* 1921: 2:40). Through statistical studies in Bengal, he developed a theory positing Indians' heightened propensity for habitual crime between the ages of twenty-five and thirty, which differed from that of Britain, where the statistical peak of recidivism was between the ages of fifteen to twenty. Concluding that the local age limit for juvenile reformatories, sixteen, was too low, he recommended that prisoners *up to thirty-five* be admitted to reformatories. Accordingly, he critiqued British penology for centering an absolute age-based cutoff for juvenility. For Mulvany, *immaturity*, not age, was the more reliable criterion for classifying (Indian) prisoners since it incorporated assessment of both physical and mental development. No doubt, such "provincial" criteria for juvenility might seem progressive for implying that older Indians be interned in reformatories. But they reified a developmentalist discourse that cast Indian same-sex relations as invariably hierarchical and violent. As scholars have noted, the scientific understanding of homosexuality in Europe shifted at the fin de siècle from connoting a pederastic, age-stratified relationship to indexing an age-proximate one (and arguably, also from sex to sexual love) (see Amin 2017; Kahan 2019). Thereby, pederasty was cast as a despotic relation that afflicted "primitive" European colonies. In this light, Mulvany's criteria for adjudicating Indian maturity allowed him to juvenilize Indians who participated in sodomy as "boys" although they were as old as thirty-five.

Indeed, such myopia prevented him from fully apprehending the intercepted missives as *love* letters at all. But as frequently as the letters contained threats, they evinced tokens of tenderness and passion. Several are solely composed as poetry:

Why does he not get the person whom he
loves?
If there be happiness in union, then when
separation comes, why does love not leave?
As the flies fall into the fire so the mind always
Runs to the object of love. . . .
[1926-B, to an adolescent convict, November 1915]

Know you Monmohan Rai that the moon has
many stars but the stars have the moon only.
So you have many but for me there is you only.
[To a fellow convict]

Written less to arrange a secret tryst than to communicate the writers' intense
attachment, such poetry recalls the Perso-Hindustani tradition of *amrad-parasti/
laundebaazi* or boy-worship/play, in which a lover expresses desire for a formulai-
cally indifferent adolescent male. Alternatively, it invokes the Hindustani/Bengali
bhakti tradition of *viraha* (romantic separation and longing). *Bhakti* highlighted
power differentials, not age hierarchies, between the feminized lover/devotee and
the capricious beloved/deity. The poetic metaphors of flies and fire, moon and
stars, are common to both, but the stilted translation makes it impossible to tell
which is referenced.

The exchange of such love letters may have extended and "spiritualized"
the courtship between some prisoners. For example:

My heart has become quite sick and sore of the world to-day. I have been
thinking for sometime that I should not work in the Press any more, but
again I made up my mind to speak to nobody. I always think of things such
as one in a frenzy thinks of. O snowy love, which made me think of many
sweet things some time before, but at last I am brittled [?]. You would have
no occasion to commit sodomy with me again, so try to secure someone else
instead. . . . Burma caught hold of [me] when I felt inclined to go to cell. . . .
When I see you I repent my follies. My doom awaits me in the cell.

      Your antagonist and adorer,

      (Sd.) ISMILE

Perhaps the most elaborate letter, this ambivalent missive is composed in a lyri-
cally affective register. Though more complex than the fragmented notes, it contains a similar meticulous sense of the prison's spatial architecture: either the

writer has been isolated or anticipates imminent separation. He identifies with a pervasive stereotype of Burmese prisoners as "recipients" and appears to have internalized Mulvany's racialized vocabulary to communicate his "brittled" self. I suggest, therefore, that the condition of the production of such letters was their writers' shared sense of mental and moral isolation. In consequence, even when they articulate poetic tropes of tragic romance in their letters, such idioms convey not just individual despair at a beloved's apathy, but also the "subject effects" of the carceral architecture housing and dividing them. After all, such missives would hardly be required if prisoners were housed in association.

My aim is not to romanticize these letters as embodying a unitary, collective "subaltern" subjectivity that predated or necessarily survived prison. Anjali Arondekar (2009) has warned historians against seeking sexuality's "truth" in the archive through the modern queer imperative of loss/recovery; such operations replay imperial hunts for "sexuality" as something to be extracted. For instance, in 1897, Ellis had solicited evidence of Indian "sexual inversion" from Mulvany's soon-to-be superior, Buchanan. Then the superintendent of Bhagalpore Jail, and before long, the editor of the *Indian Medical Gazette*, Buchanan wielded enormous authority as an arbiter of biomedicine and penology, but he categorically denied "inversion's" existence; later, he also prevented the publication of Mulvany's research in the *Gazette*. Unsurprisingly, then, Ellis (1915: 21) complained that "the real invert, if he exists" among non-Europeans, "passes unperceived." Yet the point is less to lament the stonewalling of a prospecting imperial sexologist than to analyze how colonial penal and sexological *technē* were geared toward preserving the colonial order through degrees of willful ignorance rather than through knowledge.

Despite Mulvany's treatment of prisoners as potentially redeemable individuals, even he appeared unmindful of their intensely personal life histories. While he earlier foregrounded anatomical symptoms of sodomy to statistically extrapolate its scope, the new evidential genre of the love letters produced in a transformed experimental setting did not lead him to a different framework for understanding sodomy. Rather, Mulvany was often baffled by the "love" between certain prisoners. For instance, he showcased a letter to one Khogendra, "the ugliest of men, and yet all the rogues of the jail were in love with this boy" (*Indian Jails Committee* 1921: 2:60). But the letter was clearly from a "fellow adolescent":

KHOGENDRA,

I told you on several occasions that if you consider me unsuited to you, you may look elsewhere for others. But this you will not do. Because of

you I was removed from the Remission system. . . . If you attempt to [obtain ganja from others], know this to be a settled fact, that I will kill you. . . .
[To Khogendra, a fellow adolescent prisoner]

While Mulvany did describe this case as "sexual inversion," his nominal use of such identitarian terminology was belied by his focus on its potential for inciting violence in prison (*Indian Jails Committee* 1921: 2:60). Similarly, while foregrounding letters may point to his concern with prisoners' voices and selves, he deployed them to claim that they were "only selections from an immense number" (407). Though love letters offered *textual* proof of same-sex attachments in prisoner's own voices that superseded *visual* anatomical investigations, they served a similar politics of speculation about the astronomical scale of prison pederasty. Consequently, if we are to believe Mulvany's claim that he endured attempts on his life due to his examinations of every man "appointed as a night watchman, night guard, and everybody else," we may read such attempts as the prison sex offender's resistance to a science that was both a racist form of colonial male sexual violence and of knowledge production—one that would separate him from his beloved.

State Habits: On Sex and Colonial Governance

Across the Jails Committee's inspections in India, anecdotes about prison pederasty accompanied ample speculation on its rampancy. But to shield Buchanan, the committee particularly discredited Mulvany's work, questioning whether it applied "to the great majority of Indian prisoners," even as it shared some of Mulvany's assumptions (*Indian Jails Committee* 1921: 1:99–100). For instance, some members backed Mulvany's speculation about the scale of prison sex because of his incontrovertible epistolary evidence: while "definite proof of such secret practices would [hardly] be common," no one "can read these letters without being impressed with grave objections" to association (115). Ultimately, the full committee came to a consensus only about cloistering "habituals" in special jails, with a 25–30 percent increase in cells for housing "prisoners suspected of sodomy" around the clock (94). While conceding that "sodomites" be isolated, however, committee members remained anxious that *ordinary* prisoners would commit sodomy in association. Consequently, they remained divided about the extent to which speculation about sodomy—while constitutive of the discursive grammar of colonial penology—would be allowed to dictate the material architecture of confinement for all prisoners.

Nowhere was this inverse relationship between evidence and speculation as pronounced as in the Andamans settlement, to which "unnatural offenders" and political prisoners were transported from Calcutta. Established in 1858 to house political prisoners after the 1857 Indian rebellion, the settlement accommodated over twelve thousand inmates by 1900, almost all of them men. This skewed sex ratio catalyzed recurrent rumors about sodomy in association barracks or jungle camps (Weston 2008). Those *shown* to be "habitual recipients" via medical examination were assigned to labor gangs that constructed the very cellular jail in 1906 in which they would later be interned, like political prisoners (Ludwig 2013). Though convictions were limited because of the "indignity in being submitted to examination," accusations of sodomy were handily resorted to by prisoners looking to settle scores; estimates of actual participants ranged from 5 percent to 25 percent of the inmate population, although precise figures were unavailable (*Indian Jails Committee* 1921: 2:319). Administrators consequently based their suspicions "on facts," such as instances in which when "a man [was] sent away to another camp, he [said] 'I must have that boy with me' [or] threaten[ed] to commit murder" (338). The testimonies of many local officers damned the penal colony, but the committee downplayed their concerns to allow the state to continue to run the settlement.

Faced with releasing Mulvany's incriminating testimony about pederasty in Bengal jails alongside his confession about falsifying reports on the psychological torture of political prisoners with state sanction—all within the same report, which documented the subjection of state prisoners to the Andamans settlement's "immoral" environment—the state delayed publication for over a year. It clandestinely circulated the report to provincial governments, anticipating that they would retain association, convict overseership, and transportation to the Andamans as standard penological procedure due to financial constraints. But beginning with the revolutionary terrorist movement in early twentieth-century Bengal, the Indian middle classes had increasingly started treating imprisonment as a national vocation, courting arrest as a badge of anticolonial protest (Mukhopadhyay 1999). Their prison memoirs ensured "that the subject [of squalid prison conditions would] be kept well to the fore."[6] The additional secretary to the Indian government, H. Williamson, feared that any report that comprised "a good deal of unpleasant reading" on sodomy as well as allegations about the sanctioned torture of political prisoners would "excite a section of the public, both British and Indian" and that "criticism may become violent."[7] So he urged against publishing the *Minutes of Evidence*—collated in four supplementary volumes of the report—where the bulk of Mulvany's evidence was "quoted at some length."[8] Nevertheless, he also recommended publishing the sanitized report itself to prevent the impression of a state coverup.

The state's fears were further stoked by a searing critique of the Andamans settlement in the *Daily Herald* by Colonel Wedgwood, a liberal member of the British Parliament. Citing the account of an ex-political convict, Bhai Parmanand, Wedgwood claimed that Burmese prisoners, about one-third of Andamans inmates, were treated as prostitutes by "border ruffians and the martial races" (Wedgwood 1920). Moreover, he alleged that prisoners from the martial races "bully political prisoners who are their especial prey," adding the inflammatory specter of the latter being exposed to sexual abuse (Wedgwood 1920). Under pressure, state officials decided that it was "impolitic to withhold [the report] altogether" and ultimately presented it in the *British* Parliament without the supplementary volumes.[9]

The frenzied correspondence on the report between the viceroy, the secretary of state, and senior government officials clearly reveals that the state sought to claim that speculation on jail sodomy was just that—speculation—even as it prevented Mulvany from publishing his evidence. Based on sexological "experiments," however improvised, Mulvany's work challenged the governmental will-not-to-know about prison sodomy because his intercepted letters offered "the most 'conclusive evidence'" of its prevalence (Mulvany 1921c). By preventing its circulation, the state bought itself time to announce that the Andamans settlement would be closing imminently, helping the matter to avoid direct scrutiny. Meanwhile, the transportation of political prisoners, women, and "unnatural offenders" to the Andamans settlement was to cease entirely as a compromise. But secreting "science" allowed the state to limit claims of the ubiquity of prison pederasty to the exceptional bounded space of the Andaman Islands, even as it continued to run the settlement covertly.

Afterlives: Scandal and the Circulations of Sexology

As historians uncover dense global networks of sexual knowledges at the turn of the twentieth century, how do we read this scandal involving a would-be prison sexologist? When the dust settled, finances, alongside concerns for order, largely continued to dictate prison architecture. Mulvany's documentation of prisoners' voices did not apparently leave any citational trail or have a lasting influence, except, perhaps, on those he incarcerated. And yet, one may ask if it was coincidental that both kinds of prisoners exposed to the spatial governance of graded confinement—political prisoners and habitual sodomites—began producing personal narratives of moral isolation and transformation in prison, whether in the form of prison memoirs or love letters. If the experimental *technē* for policing the sodomite and the political prisoner were informed by each other, both (but differently) in Bengal and the Andamans, as I show, then it is not far-fetched to argue that their life histories informed each other even if they were not always in intimate contact.[10] How, one could ask, are the prison auto/biographies of contemporary "ascetic" revolutionaries haunted by the secreted figure of the prison sodomite/ pederast whose presence they too often obscure?[11]

Aside from highlighting the fact that neither doctor-scientist nor patient-prisoner in India conformed to the prescriptions of European sexology, the scandal of prison pederasty shows that science, speculation, ignorance, and sexual/political subjectivity in the colony were inextricably dependent on each other, rendering geopolitics central to how sexological knowledge circulated. Histories of sexology might then visiblize how circulation is constituted by stasis and coagulation, deferred recognition, and diverse temporalities (Mulholland 2018). The intended short-circuiting of colonial prison sexology's currency within and beyond "global" sexual science consequently merits as much investigation as its subterranean successes in engendering new forms of sexual/political life.

Notes

1. Mulvany used the terms *sodomy* and *pederasty* interchangeably in his work, the reasons for which I explain later in the essay.
2. For a related take on US penology, see Kunzel 2006.
3. Elsewhere, I document the racist rectal symptomatology of sodomy/pederasty that emerged from medico-legal anatomical examinations. See Sequeira 2022 and Arondekar 2009.
4. All letters are drawn from "Appendix III" and "V" (*Indian Jails Committee 1919–20*, 2:402–10).
5. *Hobson-Jobson: The Anglo-Indian Dictionary*, s.v. "*chokra*," https://dsal.uchicago.edu /cgi-bin/app/hobsonjobson_query.py?qs=CHOKRA&searchhws=yes.
6. *The Indian Jails Committee 1919–20, Departmental Notes and Appendices*, P&J1911/1924.
7. "Minute," January 1, 1921. J&P 8899/1920 and 222/1921 in *The Indian Jails Committee Report*; *Government of India Letters to Local Government*, IOR/L/PJ/6/1683.
8. "Minute," January 1, 1921.
9. *The Indian Jails Committee 1919–20, Departmental Notes and Appendices*, P&J1911/1924.
10. For an account of middle-class revolutionary autobiographies, see Ghosh 2017.

11. For instance, the incoming inspector-general of Bengal Prisons claimed that "sodomy is part of the initiation ceremony in one of [Bengal's] political clubs" (*Indian Jails Committee* 1921: 1:113). Also see Silvestri 2019: 55.

References

Amin, Kadji. 2017. *Disturbing Attachments: Genet, Modern Pederasty, and Queer History.* Durham, NC: Duke University Press.

Anderson, Clare. 2004. *Legible Bodies: Race, Criminality, and Colonialism in South Asia.* Oxford, UK: Berg.

Arnold, David. 1992. *Colonizing the Body: State Medicine and Epidemic Disease in Nineteenth-Century India.* Berkeley: University of California Press.

Arnold, David. 1994. "The Colonial Prison: Power, Knowledge, and Penology in Nineteenth-Century India." In *Subaltern Studies VIII*, 148–84. New Delhi: Oxford University Press.

Arondekar, Anjali. 2009. *For the Record: On Sexuality and the Archive in Colonial India.* Durham, NC: Duke University Press.

Buchanan, W. (1898) 1900. *A Manual of Jail Hygiene.* Calcutta: Bengal Secretariat Press.

Ellis, Havelock. (1897) 1915. *Sexual Inversion.* Philadelphia, PA: F. A. Davis and Company.

Foucault, Michel. 1978. *The History of Sexuality: Volume I*, translated by Robert Hurley. New York: Pantheon Books.

Indian Jails Committee, 1919–20. 1921. 5 vols. Calcutta: Superintendent Government Printing, India.

Kahan, Benjamin. 2019. *The Book of Minor Perverts: Sexology, Etiology, and the Emergences of Sexuality.* Chicago: University of Chicago Press.

Kunzel, Regina. 2006. *Criminal Intimacy: Prison and the Uneven History of Modern American Sexuality.* Chicago: University of Chicago Press.

Ludwig, Manju. 2013. "Murder in the Andamans: A Colonial Narrative of Sodomy, Jealousy and Violence." *South Asia Multidisciplinary Academic Journal.* https://doi.org/10.4000/samaj.3633.

Mukhopadhyay, Anindita. 1999. "Jail Darpan: The Image of the Jail in Bengali Middle-Class Literature." *Studies in History* 15, no. 1: 109–44.

Mulholland, James. 2018. "An Indian It-Narrative and the Problem of Circulation: Reconsidering a Useful Concept for Literary Study." *Modern Language Quarterly* 79, no. 4: 373–96.

Mulvany, John. 1921a. "Appendix IX: Recidivism and Immorality in Bengal Jails." In *Indian Jails Committee* 1921: 2:411–13.

Mulvany, John. 1921b. "Appendix X: Copies of Correspondence Relating to the Treatment of State Prisoners." In *Indian Jails Committee* 1921: 2:413–14.

Mulvany, John. 1921c. "To the Editor." *Times of India*, August 3.

Puri, Jyoti. 2017. *Sexual States: Governance and the Struggle over Antisodomy Law in India*. Durham, NC: Duke University Press.

Report on the Administration of the Andaman and Nicobar Islands and the Penal Settlement of Port Blair, 1907–08. 1908. Calcutta: Office of the Superintendent Government Printing.

Sen, Satadru. 2000. *Disciplining Punishment: Colonialism and Convict Society in the Andaman Islands*. New Delhi: Oxford University Press.

Sequeira, Rovel. 2022. "Don't Ask, Won't Tell? Sexual Science and the Case Biography of Sodomy in Colonial India." *Modernism/modernity* 29, no. 1: 145–68.

Silvestri, Michael. 2019. *Policing Bengali Terrorism in India and the World: Imperial Intelligence and Revolutionary Nationalism, 1905–1939*. Basingstoke, UK: Palgrave Macmillan.

Sinha, Mrinalini. 1995. *Colonial Masculinity: The "Manly" Englishman and the "Effeminate" Bengali*. Manchester, UK: Manchester University Press.

Waits, Mira Rai. 2018. "Imperial Vision, Colonial Prisons: British Jails in Bengal, 1823–73." *Journal of the Society of Architectural Historians* 77, no. 2: 146–67.

Wedgwood, Josiah IV. 1920. "Hell in the Andamans." *Daily Herald*, December 29.

Weston, Kath. 2008. "A Political Ecology of 'Unnatural Offences': State Security, Queer Embodiment, and the Environmental Impacts of Prison Migration." *GLQ* 14, nos. 2–3: 217–37.

Yang, Anand. 1985. *Crime and Criminality in British India*. Tucson: University of Arizona Press.

THE SECRETS
OF A LOYALIST SOUL

Psychoanalysis and Homosexuality in Wartime China

Howard Chiang

*I*n the autumn of 1937, two men crossed paths in the neuropsychiatric ward of Peking Union Medical College (PUMC).[1] One of them, Li, was a young college student, twenty-two years old and married. He came from a lower middle-class family and a region occupied by the Japanese. In Beijing, where he had been living and attending school for the previous six years, Li had had sexual relations with both men and women.[2] A patriot once imprisoned and tortured by the Japanese, Li surprisingly began to learn Japanese, made Japanese friends, and even decided to work for the puppet regime in the former Chinese capital. The other, Bingham Dai 戴秉衡 (1899–1996), received his PhD in sociology at the University of Chicago and was a professor of medical psychology. Before assuming his post at PUMC, Dai had learned about the culture-and-personality school at Yale University, undergone analysis with the neo-Freudianist Harry Stack Sullivan (1892–1949) in New York, and become the first Chinese to practice psychoanalysis in northern China in the 1930s (Blowers 2004; Wang 2006; Rose 2009; Huang 2020). Dai saw Li for seventy-one sessions over the course of ten months. Their treatment aimed to uncover Li's unconscious thoughts and relieve his obsessive-compulsive neurosis.

Li's chief complaint concerned his compulsive thinking of a hairy paw of some animal—later revealed to be a black bear, a symbol of Japanese imperialism that he had learned in childhood—and his constant fear of a male figure, both approaching him from behind. These thoughts were preceded by a gradual increase of irritability, feverishness, palpitation of the heart, shortness of breath, and flushing of the face, especially acute when coming into contact with the Japanese. The symptoms had worsened exponentially since the onset of the formal Japanese invasion of China in 1937. The fear of the hairy paw and the imagi-

GLQ 29:1
DOI 10.1215/10642684-10144407

nary man—which caused him to look back anxiously and uncontrollably—dated from the time when the Japanese occupied Beijing that summer. Later in therapy, Li revealed a secondary set of symptoms that involved obsessively looking at and touching objects four times, especially holes, dark spots, and empty spaces such as inside a drawer or underneath a bed. Dai considered the two sets of symptoms interrelated and concluded that his analysis of Li ultimately provided a fresh perspective on the psychology of Quislingism, that is, the question of why an individual would willingly cooperate with the enemy in the context of war. It made sense, Dai reasoned, for Li's neurosis to deteriorate as the Japanese approached his place of residence.

Although Li's case may seem to center on the theme of divided loyalty, or so Dai claimed, it was in fact saturated with queer overtones. For instance, Dai (1944: 331) noted that as a child, "Li has been greatly interested in a sexual manner not only in his mother but in his father." In one of the interviews, Li related his desire to relocate to Free China in the south to his dream of being arrested by a Japanese who "moved a hairy piece of metal in and out of his anus" (332). In another session, Li recalled dreaming about a Japanese teacher searching his room and, on the following day, "a strong man getting on top of him under a bed" (333). On a third night, before falling asleep "he found himself compulsively thinking of having sexual relations with the Japanese teacher" (333). And then in several incidences of what psychotherapists would identify as the phenomenon of transference, Li expressed thoughts of having passive homosexual relations with the analyst, that is, Dai himself. In a highly eroticized dream, Dai asked Li to take off his clothes in the hospital and reactivated one of Li's childhood fantasies in which he was sexually penetrated by a dog (336). Again, it is remarkable that Dai's takeaway from all of this—somewhere between the clinic, the military, and the school— was not the problem of sexual perversion, but Li's collaboration with the Japanese.

The fact that Dai did not isolate Li's homosexuality as the overarching analytical issue suggests that for Dai, more was at stake than the patient's psychosexual conflicts. As we will see, this bears wider implications about Dai's approach to psychoanalysis and the ways in which psychodynamic techniques were implemented at PUMC, at the time the most prestigious teaching hospital in China funded by the Rockefeller Foundation (fig. 1) (Bullock 1980). In a country where Sigmund Freud's ideas had been widely discussed, translated, and troped in fiction, Dai's analytical orientation can be summarized in four words: Freud was not enough (Zhang 1992; Larson 2009). Although the dominant psychoanalytic literature on homosexuality is replete with the tension between pathologization and normalization, the Dai-Li episode casts an alternative light on the interrelation

Figure 1. Medical staff of the neuropsychiatric unit at the Peking Union Medical College (1936). Bingham Dai is the fourth from the right in the second row, next to Richard R. Lyman, who directed the unit and recruited Dai both to PUMC in the 1930s and Duke University School of Medicine in the 1940s. Bingham Dai Papers, Photo Album, 1934–1946, PUMC staff, Box 41, RB 8007. Courtesy of Special Collections, Appalachian State University.

between psychoanalysis and the sexual drive (Lewes 1988). Unfolding in a non-Western clinical setting, Dai's treatment of Li shows how psychoanalysis can operate as a powerful tool to denaturalize the concept of homosexuality itself. With the principal aim of helping the patient reach a balanced state of social functioning, Dai's analysis parses homoerotic tendencies less in terms of sexual instinct per se than as a symptom of personality conflicts and cultural (mal)adjustments. Dai's countertransference in the clinic further raises questions about his own biographical and subjective attachment, as well as about the instability of sexual meaning in the therapeutic encounter. For his method to work, Dai needed—and indeed developed—a new style of scientific reasoning rooted in a transcultural frame.

Departing from Freud

Dai's departure from Freud rests on an interpretive emphasis of the human as a social being rather than a purely biological one. Freud's libido theory construed the sexual drive as the most organic origin of motivation and behavior; therefore, Freudians sought to unlock the hidden processes of psychic dynamics *inside* the individual. In contrast, Dai's analytical orientation resembled the interpersonal approach of his mentor, Sullivan, which attempted to contextualize a patient's interest within a social relational network. How the patient interacted—or wanted to interact—*with others* mattered. As Stephen Mitchell and Margaret Black (2016: 63) put it, "whereas the Freudian analyst is looking for repressed wishes and fantasies, Sullivan is looking for unattended interactions."

Quislingism, the focus of Dai's study, presents a clear example of this difference. In the classic Freudian impression, the term came from Ernest Jones and was associated with the Nazis. In "The Psychology of Quislingism," Jones (1941) interpreted the patients' reaction to Hitlerism as an identification with the formidable father figure. They registered the demands of the Nazis as "the Father's demanding back the penis of which he had been robbed" (5). The familiar Oedipus complex, or early sexual rivalry between father and son, became the explanation for a later life situation. On first consideration, this reading may seem equally suitable for the Li case. As Dai noted, many episodes in Li's life might substantiate the presence of an Oedipus complex. Not only did Li repeatedly claim incestuous desires toward his mother, but he also sought to resolve his fear of and hatred for his father through castration desires and homosexual relations. "In his associations," Dai (1944: 335) noted, "[Li] said that when he had sexual thoughts about his mother he often wished to castrate himself." However, in the same paragraph, Dai distanced himself from Freud by insisting that sexual motivation served a larger purpose: "The patient considered a homosexual attack upon himself not only as a form of love relationship but as a means of punishment as well" (335). In other words, the analyst was moving away from the argument that earlier Oedipus conflicts simply remained dormant until being reactivated by later thoughts, such as the unconscious identification of the enemy with the father.

Instead of viewing the patient as a biological being, Dai preferred a more "social personality" approach. "Instinctual conflicts are not to be ignored," Dai qualified, "but are to be understood in the context of interpersonal relations" (337). In practice, this meant identifying the patient's primary self as formed in his primary group environment, typically the natal family, versus the other conceptions of a self that matured later in life (Dai 1931, 1939, 1952). In Li's case, Dai examined his primary personality formation through his family background and upbringing, followed by juxtaposing this self-concept with the way Li adjusted to the social conditions of Japanese occupation. The magnitude of his neurosis varied "according to the extent to which a person's basic and generally unconscious conceptions

of himself or roles precipitated by his primary group experiences during his formative years come into conflict with his more recent and more rational conceptions of
himself acquired in the course of later social contacts" (Dai 1944: 337–38). Li's
mental duress in the present became a problem of interpersonal relations, and his
conflicts with the Japanese were no more symbolic than the actual conflicts with
his own father. In this way, Dai displaced the conflict between the id and superego
in Freudian psychoanalysis in favor of the dissidence between two or more self-
images, seizing this dissidence to conceptualize the basis of personality organization and development.

In order to explore the interactional dynamics between distinct self-images
and reach back to Li's early childhood experience, Dai developed a transcultural
style of reasoning. This epistemic style debunks the assumption that Western biomedical categories are universally applicable, treats thinking across geographical
and disciplinary borders as the basis of evidence, generates new categories and
parameters of scientific inquiry, and repositions its practitioners from the margin to
the center of scholarly discourses (Chiang 2021). Chinese cultural factors anchored
Dai's deciphering of the Li case. For instance, the preference for a male child in
Chinese families offered an important clue to Li's primary self-formation. As the
only son, Li was constantly spoiled by his parents and relatives. His father would
not allow his mother to punish him until he was five years old, and his grandparents
would go behind his parents' backs to give him whatever he wanted. Thus, Dai
(1944: 331) considered it understandable that "such a child might develop a greed
for love and affection." Another important element of the Chinese family structure
was the norm, especially in northern China, for the entire family to sleep together
on one big bed, or *kang*. In Dai's view, this meant "one might anticipate an early
development of this child's erotic interest in his parents" (331). Moreover, the Confucian emphasis on filial piety disparaged the acting out of aggressive impulses,
especially toward elders. This of course did not mean that the child held no grudges
toward authority figures, but the child would need to find other ways to cope with
his hostile impulses. In Li's case, Dai reported that "the patient had developed
the habit of slapping himself whenever severely scolded by his mother, and later
showed the same reaction pattern even in his relation with girl friends" (331).

Adjusting the Primal Scene

By integrating Chinese cultural mores into dream analysis, Dai (329) unraveled
an original scene in which trauma was produced and with which psychoanalysis
began:

> When Li was about six he was one day quarreling with a boy in the neigh-
> borhood; and as he was going to hit the playmate with an ax, his father
> suddenly kicked him from behind and gave him a very severe shock. Since
> then, he said, he had frequent nightmares up to the age of 16, during which
> he would yell out and said that his father had been killed. These night-
> mares were also accompanied by what he described as slight feverishness,
> shortness of breath, palpitation of heart and profuse sweating.

This episode epitomized the roots of Li's fear and fantasy, both manifested in the
form of something, or someone, approaching him from behind. In fact, Chinese
cultural norms are important because they offer a context for acknowledging the
severity of Li's aggressive impulses. In Chinese culture, explained Dai (331), "hostile acts, as a rule, are totally banned, no matter whether the child himself is in
the right or the wrong." Li's intention to hurt a playmate with an ax was considered
so severe and intolerable that his father, who would ordinarily keep his wife from
physically punishing Li, decided to do so himself. This childhood trauma came to
serve as the baseline against which Li's later desires and behaviors were calibrated
in therapy.

For ten months, Dai decoded the underlying meaning of Li's dreams by
returning to this primal scene more than once.[3] For example, when Li told Dai that
he dreamt of being caught by a Japanese man who inserted a hairy piece of metal
into his anus, Dai claimed that this dream "dramatized his secretly preferred but
strongly repressed way of coming to terms with the enemy, submitting to a homosexual attack by the Japanese, a pattern of adjustment naturally unacceptable to
a college student conscious only of love for his country and hatred of the enemy"
(332). The Japanese became in the 1930s what Li's father meant to him at six: an
enemy, loathed and dreaded, attacking him from behind. Dai *superimposed* homosexual fantasy *and* the feelings of fear/hatred toward the enemy onto one another,
and in so doing, he rendered the forming of same-sex relations as a displaced effort
on the part of the patient to adjust to the conditions of Japanese occupation.

As an adult, Li had numerous dreams filled with homoerotic content. He
recalled being sexually obsessed with his Japanese teacher, "vaguely and reluctantly thought of having passive sex relations with [a lizard, which] made him think
of the bear and of Mussolini," and wanted to engage in sexual relations with his
father (333). "On the basis of such materials," Dai (333) deduced, "one can no
longer doubt that the patient was attempting unconsciously to establish a passive
emotional relationship with the enemy, expressed in homosexual terms, and that
the pattern was set in his formative period in the course of his relationship with

his father." Unlike the classical dream analysis exemplified by Freud's (1918) Wolf Man, these later dreams are less exemplary of an original childhood trauma enigmatic to the patient; rather, they are a tool that enabled the analyst to bridge the interpersonal conflicts from the past with the present. The impulses and wishes of the past (the emphasis of classical Freudianism) became only a partial segment of larger interpersonal configurations. In Dai's view, Li's homosexuality was less a cause than a symptom of a more underlying psychic structure: forming allegiance based on the feeling of repulsion toward the enemy. The cultural pillar of this psychic structure can be located in the evolving contours of Sino-Japanese relations.

The Cultural Interpretation of Dreams

Dai (1941, 1957) espoused the significance of cultural sensitivity in order to achieve a complete picture of the patient's problem and the ideal solution to it. For Dai to pursue his interest in Chinese culture and personality, knowledge of the Chinese language was necessary and decisive. In fact, as Dai would later concede, the case that instigated his interest in dream analysis was that of an illiterate seventeen-year-old Chinese girl. She visited PUMC to complain about her irrational fear of being sexually attacked by a dog. On the surface, her problem appeared sexual in origin, and orthodox Freudians might trace her fantasy back to an early disturbance in psychosexual development. But Dai patiently inquired about the girl's dream, which took the form of a beggar picking up a lump of coal from the street. The girl said the beggar made her think of "the old man in the moon" (*yuelao*), which is a Chinese god responsible for matchmaking. In Beijing, the word for "coal" is pronounced *mei*, which could mean either the fuel for cooking or matchmaking (though the Chinese characters for these two words are different, their pronunciation is identical). This convinced Dai that what the girl unconsciously desired was to get married. Dai (1979: 33) later recalled that "this uneducated patient's dream with its poetic representation of her inner knowledge of her own problem made a very deep impression on me." Though this teenage girl's story cemented Dai's commitment to dream analysis, his approach to dreams differed from Freud's interpretive mode, especially with respect to the ample leverage for self-knowledge and explanation that Dai granted his patients.

Resting on this legacy, Chinese linguistic competence played a determinant role in Dai's analysis of Li, especially the connection between his compulsive obsessive behavior and his interpersonal relations with women. Dai traced Li's obsession with touching objects four times, which began at the age of eighteen, to the Chinese word for "four," *si*. This word made Li think of the familiar phrase "peace and quiet in all four seasons" (*siji ping'an*) and death, because in Li's dialect, the Chinese word for death, *si*, was pronounced practically the same as the word for four (Dai 1944: 329–30). In one of his interviews, Li "associated this compulsive behavior with his interest in mother's genitalia" and "his early erotic interest in . . . other female relatives of the family" (329). The foremost test for Li's love/hate relationship with his parents—both his father and his mother—came with a marriage they arranged for him at the age of fifteen, with a girl to whom he felt no connection (330). After he left his wife behind in his hometown and arrived in Beijing by himself the following year, he began to sleep with both older and younger women, some of whom he impregnated. Thus, Li's relationship with women was at once intense and fleeting, always resulting in a certain sense of guilt. Treating women as mother substitutes, Li often demanded sexual intercourse with girlfriends (though not his left-behind wife) after hostile encounters with the Japanese. Li would show obedience to the Japanese during those uncomfortable confrontations but would subsequently have sex with his female partners (but again, not with his wife) "like a hungry child being fed" (334). In the final analysis, Dai concluded that "women . . . could serve only as buffers or scapegoats in the patient's encounter with a threatening situation; they could neither take the place of a direct settlement with the enemy nor provide a satisfactory resolution of the hostile impulses continually aroused by his presence and their accompanying fear of punishment" (334–35). In the language of relational psychoanalysis, female partners became intermediary "objects" that Li used to cope with his psychic distress.

The primal scene continued to serve as a touchpoint for later connections. Li's recourse to passive homosexual relations, as evident in his numerous dream episodes, became the hallmark of his social adjustment in time of war. In Dai's analytical framework, although homosexual and heterosexual impulses are both important, what mattered most was the patient's actualization of a self that allowed him to be consistent with his personality as a whole (Dai 1981). The principal aim of their sessions was not to treat Li's homosexuality, or bisexuality as the case may be, but to bring into Li's consciousness his hidden psychological mechanisms for dealing with the Japanese. In Beijing, Li sought protection by the Japanese, under which he could secretly carry out anti-Japanese activities. Dai (1944: 333) observed that "as such desires became more and more conscious thoughts, his symptoms subsided, until by the thirty-third interview, he said that 95 per cent of his symptoms had disappeared."

Homo Transference

When historians explore the relationship between psychoanalysis and homosexuality, they typically interpret this dialectical relation in a singular frame, with the former serving as the subject and the latter the object of historical action. In other words, critics have preoccupied themselves with how analysts viewed homosexuality in the past and how those theoretical perspectives changed over time (Lewes 1988; Terry 1999). Yet no less profound is the question of *how psychoanalysis and psychoanalysts can be queered* through their clinical engagement with homosexuality (Fuss 1995; Herzog 2020). As historian John Forrester (2017: 65) has shown, the psychoanalytic case presents a puzzling zone of contact—between the analyst and the analysand, on the one hand, and the author and the reader, on the other: "It is the privileged means for attempting to convey the unique psychoanalytic experience of *both* patient and analyst."

As a science and a form of art, like most branches of medicine, psychoanalysis cuts both ways by objectifying and subjectifying itself. Yet the key to psychoanalytic writing takes the form of a betrayal. Such textualization betrays its function to uncover the hidden, concealed truth at the very moment when it is subjected to the same laws and processes of the psychoanalytic scenario itself. To quote Forrester's (66) eloquent formulation, the pertinent questions about the epistemic stakes of the psychoanalytic project are: "Should [the psychoanalyst] fight the good fight for objectivity, thus depriving psychoanalysis of its own logic, pretending that it is something other than it is? Or should she brave the sceptic and undress—as far as she dare—in public, because any other way would be to pretend that she is not naked underneath the respectable clothes of professional everyday life and would deny that nakedness is the point of wearing clothes in the first place?"

This predicament recognizes the psychoanalytic encounter as a highly charged, intensely emotional, and deeply personal event. This is indicative in the Dai-Li dynamic because, as his terminal but foremost psychoanalytic evidence, Dai presented and scrutinized the patient's transference of attachment, fantasies, and desire onto the analyst in detail. Dai (1944: 335) defined transference as a phenomenon in which "the patient as a rule tends to act toward the analyst much in the same way as he does toward other people significant in his current life situation, and especially as he did toward those who made up his early social environment." In their initial meetings, Li would bow twice when entering and leaving Dai's office and would rush to light Dai's cigarette. Yet these overcourteous gestures were simply a defense mechanism for how Li felt deep down inside. Over time, Li apologized for the possibility of coming off as being impolite to the analyst and even explicitly noted the resemblance between listening to Dai and the feeling of being scolded by his own father. This identification of Dai with Li's father carried over into Li's dreams. In his dreams, Li not only desired a passive homosexual relation with Dai (and a dog, from his childhood fantasy) but also lived in the hospital with a version of the analyst who was "taller and larger than in reality and that his hands were as strong and as rough as those of his father" (336).

Upon reflecting on these dreams, Li maintained an ambivalent attitude toward Dai, both respectful and hostile (at one point, Li wished to behead Dai). The homosexual dreams, then, became his passive-aggressive solution to the contemporary discomfort, in line with his "retreating without a fight" approach when dealing with elders as a child and the Japanese as an adult. In conclusion, Dai (336) remarked that "through an intensive study of this situation, the patient came to see that his attitude toward the analyst was in many ways similar to his attitude toward the Japanese and that both contained components that really did not belong to the present situation: they came from the attitudes that he had acquired during his formative years in the course of his relationship with his parents, especially his father." Dai's utilization of transference was intended to synchronize the various versions of the self that Li had developed over the course of his life and to highlight and smooth the fissures between them. Through such an endeavor, Li could gain a better sense of his personality organization and, by extension, adjust it to strive for better social functioning in the present.

(De)Coding Countertransference

But is that all that this psychoanalytic case is about? What can be said about Dai's own attachment—to psychoanalysis, of course, but also issues of sexuality (homosexuality/heterosexuality) and nationalism (patriotism/Quislingism)? The history of how Dai came to be acquainted with psychoanalysis offers an indispensable hint of Dai's own countertransference in the Li case. Although primarily trained in the Chicago school of sociology, Dai attended a life-changing seminar at Yale in 1932. The seminar was titled "The Impact of Culture on Personality," convened by anthropologist Edward Sapir (1884–1939), and brought together thirteen students of different disciplines and cultural backgrounds to explore the intersection between psychiatry and social science (Dai 1932). At the Yale seminar, Dai was impressed by the neo-Freudian approach of one of the seminar speakers, Harry Stack Sullivan, whose emphasis on interpersonal relations resonated with Dai's interest in Confucian social norms and familial dynamics (Dai 1982–1983: 13).

Awed by this epistemological resonance, Dai decided to undergo analysis with Sullivan, his first psychoanalytic mentor, in New York.

Though all of this predated Dai's meeting with Li by five years, at the time of the Yale seminar, China's northeastern frontier, most notably Manchuria, was already becoming a puppet state of Japan. Japan's imperial ambitions had intensified, rather than diminished, after the First Sino-Japanese War (1894–1895). In a later interview conducted with his student, Dai revealed his own feelings toward the Japanese in the 1930s: "Do you know what the Japanese thought? They invade China in order to superior their relation to China. That came out of inferiority feelings, because they learn everything from China. They have a deep inferiority feeling on the part of Japanese whenever they meet Chinese. There is a great urge to prove they are equal if not superior to the Chinese. Very much like Germans" (Atkins 1986: 17). This attitude toward the Japanese served as the backdrop for Dai's experience at Yale:

> I had a funny experience with a fellow member of this Yale seminar. . . .
> There were thirteen young specialists from different cultures assembled to
> study the impact of culture upon personality. . . . One of them is Japanese.
> He tried to be very cultural and polite, but boy, was he hostile. Not hostile
> in a real way but just in a peculiar manner. One time we were discussing
> Confucius. He said, Confucius was not Chinese. Because they also adore
> Confucius. . . . They don't think of Confucius as Chinese. Chinese are
> inferior to them. . . . This is a Ph.D., in sociology. At that time the Japanese
> were entering Manchuria. . . . So he had to defend them. Even though he
> knows better. When you are under the influence of patriotism, nationalism,
> you're blind. You don't think well. He had to defend the military adventure, and yet he didn't know how to defend. And yet we had to live together
> and meet together in the seminar and discuss big problems together. A fun
> age. (18)

By the time Dai and Li connected in 1937, the threat of Japanese military aggression had become a reality in Beijing. Therefore, it is not going too far to conclude that Dai's training in and practice of psychoanalysis had been intertwined with his attitude toward Japan from the start. Was the real object of Dai's psychoanalytic investment Li's Quislingism, or his own patriotism? To the extent that countertransference has been recognized as a risk implicated in all analytical situations, what stakes does the task of treating a homosexual analysand hold for the presumably heterosexual analyst?

One can argue that instead of a novel style of science rooted in transcultural reasoning, what Dai's work advanced was a kind of self-Orientalization. Sapir selected him for the Yale seminar to represent Chinese culture, so Dai's Western peers *already* perceived him in Orientalist terms (Atkins n.d.: 4). It is possible to situate within this genealogy Dai's synthesis of Confucianism, Daoism, and Buddhism with psychotherapy (especially after his relocation to North Carolina in the 1940s). At the same time, one must not overlook the profound challenges with which Dai's positionality—as an émigré scientist, a cultural broker, and a racialized figure in a profession largely dominated by white practitioners—was infused. On the one hand, he sought to convince Chinese experts and nonexperts alike of the value of psychoanalysis. On the other, he tried to persuade Western interlocutors to listen carefully to and understand Chinese humanistic philosophy. Dai's positionality was in fact *doubly* marginalized. So, to interpret the invocation of something like Confucianism as a symbol of Orientalism is plausible, but it is equally difficult to discern where the genuineness of that interest begins or ends. I suggest treating these as two opposite ends of a historical spectrum, on which Dai's subjectivity glided according to context and contingency.

The fact that Dai published his report of Li in an Anglophone journal, *Psychiatry: Interpersonal and Biological Processes*, raises the question of intent. More specifically, did he intentionally fashion an Orientalist brand of psychodynamic science so that Li's case could be instrumentalized to market himself in the biomedical community? An affirmative response to this question lies within the stretch of imagination. Yet when Dai's career is taken into consideration from a comprehensive viewpoint, one notices that this was neither the first nor the last time he published his findings in a Western journal. In fact, this publication fits a larger pattern in which Dai consistently communicated his findings to a global readership. By acknowledging that the 1944 text denotes a web of relations in which Dai and Li, Chinese and Western intellectual traditions, and the dynamics of transference and countertransference were immersed and circulated, it is possible to bring into focus the *technical* details of his transcultural science. This would take Dai's contributions on their own terms without always having to be routed through purely Western frames of cultural reference. This also repositions Dai from the margin to the core of a scholarly discourse emerging at a time when the face of psychoanalysis was changing rapidly.

With respect to homosexuality, the psychoanalytic case examined in this essay is best situated at the crossroads of various historiographical threads. On the one hand, it follows the tendency for psychoanalysis since Freud to distance itself from the field of sexology (Sulloway 1979; Sutton 2019). In so doing, counterintuitively, psychoanalysis consolidated the very concept of homosexuality, defined it in terms of object choice (rather than aim or degeneration), and crystallized it from the earlier notion of sexual inversion, a pivotal concept in fin-de-siècle sexology (Makari 2008: 110–18). Dai never identified himself as a sexologist but spoke of homosexuality as if it was already a widely accepted concept in China (Chiang 2018: 125–77). On the other hand, the Li case follows the motivation among psychoanalysts to define their discipline as an independent field of study. In this line of pursuit, they actually denaturalized the very concept of homosexuality by arguing that sexual desires always come with a deeper set of psychic meanings and serve a larger purpose (Davidson 1987). Li's homosexual tendencies were important to Dai to the extent that they helped illuminate the analytical material about self-actualization and personality organization.

By the same token, the Dai-Li encounter captures the way politics both inhibits the development of psychoanalysis in certain parts of the world and determines its growth in other regions (Damousi and Plotkin 2012; ffytche and Pick 2016; Herzog 2017). In the 1930s, authoritarian Germany and Russia followed the former vector of psychoanalytic development, and Britain and the United States the latter. What about China? What about other non-Western societies? Dai's psychoanalytic career is only beginning to point us to some possible ways of answering these questions.

I have been arguing that the conclusion to Li's therapy does not rest solely on the transference of his desires, but also upon the countertransference of Dai's attachment. After all, Dai, the straight and cosmopolitan analyst, left China in 1939 and became a faculty member of Duke University School of Medicine in 1943; Li, the queer and passive-aggressive analysand, stayed behind in Beijing and collaborated with the Japanese just as the Asia–Pacific War entered its most virulent phase. If the true focus of their sessions, as Dai claimed, had been Quislingism and not sexual perversion, whose therapeutic interest does such a disavowal serve?

Notes

Research for this study is supported by a Dean's Faculty Fellowship from the College of Letters and Science at the University of California, Davis, a Henry Luce Fellowship from the National Humanities Center, and a research grant (RG001-A-19) from the Chiang Ching-kuo Foundation for International Scholarly Exchange. I thank Benjamin Kahan, Greta LaFleur, and the two reviewers for their helpful feedback. Any remaining errors are my own.

1.　For a history of the neuropsychiatric ward at PUMC, see Shapiro 1995; Shapiro 2014a; Shapiro 2014b; and Baum 2018. The psychoanalytic case examined in this article comes from Dai 1944.

2.　Although I adopt the word Beijing in this essay, the city, to be historically accurate, had been renamed Beiping because Chiang Kai-shek's Nationalist government relocated its capital from Nanjing to Chongqing in 1937. The renaming of Beijing to Beiping made it unambiguous to the world that the city was not China's capital during the Nationalist era. To make it easier to comprehend for readers not familiar with Chinese history, however, I have retained the anachronistic usage of Beijing in this article.

3.　Analysts like Freud and Melanie Klein use the concept of the *primal scene* to refer specifically to the child's witness of, or projection of fantasies about, parental sexual relations. Here I am borrowing the term loosely and adapting it to refer to the primary scene I discuss in this section.

References

Atkins, Sally. 1986. "Interview with Dr. Dai." April 10. Typescript. Box 39, folder 2, Bingham Dai Papers, Belk Library, Appalachian State University, Boone, NC.

Atkins, Sally. n.d. "Interview with Dr. Dai 1 of 3." Box 39, folder 5, Bingham Dai Papers, Belk Library, Appalachian State University, Boone, NC.

Baum, Emily. 2018. *The Invention of Madness: State, Society, and the Insane in Modern China*. Chicago: University of Chicago Press.

Blowers, Geoffrey. 2004. "Bingham Dai, Adolf Storfer, and the Tentative Beginnings of Psychoanalytic Culture in China, 1935–1941." *Psychoanalysis and History* 6, no. 1: 93–105.

Bullock, Mary B. 1980. *An American Transplant: The Rockefeller Foundation and Peking Union Medical College*. Berkeley: University of California Press.

Chiang, Howard. 2018. *After Eunuchs: Science, Medicine, and the Transformation of Sex in Modern China*. New York: Columbia University Press.

Chiang, Howard. 2021. "Translators of the Soul: Bingham Dai, Pow-Meng Yap, and the Making of Transcultural Psychoanalysis in the Asia Pacific." *Psychoanalysis and History* 23, no. 2: 161–85.

Dai, Bingham. 1931. "The Growth of the Self." Typescript. Box 3, folder 6, Bingham Dai Papers, Belk Library, Appalachian State University, Boone, NC.

Dai, Bingham. 1932. "Diary of the Seminar of the Impact of Culture Upon Personality." Typescript. Box 1, folder 5, Bingham Dai Papers, Belk Library, Appalachian State University, Boone, NC.

Dai, Bingham. 1939. "The Patient as a Person." In *Social and Psychological Studies in Neuropsychiatry in China*, edited by Richard S. Lyman, V. Maeker, and P. Liang, 1–30. Peking: Henri Vetch.

Dai, Bingham. 1941. "Personality Problems in Chinese Culture." *American Sociological Review* 6, no. 5: 688–96.

Dai, Bingham. 1944. "Divided Loyalty in War: A Study of Coöperation with the Enemy." *Psychiatry: Interpersonal and Biological Processes* 7, no. 4: 327–40.

Dai, Bingham. 1952. "A Socio-Psychiatric Approach to Personality Organization." *American Sociological Review* 17, no. 1: 44–49.

Dai, Bingham. 1957. "Obsessive-Compulsive Disorders in Chinese Culture." *Social Problems* 4, no. 4: 313–21.

Dai, Bingham. 1979. "My Experience of Psychotherapy: Some Reasons for My Relative Freedom from Fatigue." *Voices: The Art and Science of Psychotherapy* 15, no. 2: 26–33.

Dai, Bingham. 1981. "Being Fully Human: A Chinese Ideal of Mental Health." *Highland Highlights* (Fall): 9–14.

Dai, Bingham. 1982–1983. "On Sullivan—His Life and Work." *William Alanson White Institute Newsletter* (Winter): 12–13.

Damousi, Joy, and Mariano Ben Plotkin, eds. 2012. *Psychoanalysis and Politics: Histories of Psychoanalysis under Conditions of Restricted Political Freedom.* New York: Oxford University Press.

Davidson, Arnold I. 1987. "How to Do the History of Psychoanalysis: A Reading of Freud's *Three Essays on the Theory of Sexuality.*" *Critical Inquiry* 13, no. 2: 252–77.

ffytche, Matt, and Daniel Pick, eds. 2016. *Psychoanalysis in the Age of Totalitarianism.* London: Routledge.

Forrester, John. 2017. *Thinking in Cases.* Cambridge, UK: Polity.

Freud, Sigmund. 1918. "From the History of an Infantile Neurosis." In *Standard Edition of the Complete Psychological Works of Sigmund Freud,* vol. 17, 7–122. London: Hogarth.

Fuss, Diana. 1995. "Pink Freud." *GLQ* 2, nos. 1–2: 1–9.

Herzog, Dagmar. 2017. *Cold War Freud: Psychoanalysis in the Age of Catastrophes.* Cambridge, UK: Cambridge University Press.

Herzog, Dagmar. 2020. "Queering Freud Differently: Radical Psychoanalysis and Ethnography in the 1970s–1980s." *Psychoanalysis and History* 22, no. 1: 1–14.

Huang, Hsuan-Ying. 2020. "The History of Psychoanalysis in China." *Psychoanalytic Inquiry* 40, no. 1: 3–15.

Jones, Ernest. 1941. "The Psychology of Quislingism." *International Journal of Psychoanalysis* 22: 1–6.

Larson, Wendy. 2009. *From Ah Q to Lei Feng: Freud and Revolutionary Spirit in 20th Century China.* Stanford, CA: Stanford University Press.

Lewes, Kenneth. 1988. *The Psychoanalytic Theory of Male Homosexuality.* New York: Simon and Schuster.

Makari, George. 2008. *Revolution in Mind: The Creation of Psychoanalysis.* New York: HarperCollins.

Mitchell, Stephen A., and Margaret J. Black. (1995) 2016. *Freud and Beyond: A History of Modern Psychoanalytic Thought*. New York: Basic Books.

Rose, Anne C. 2009. *Psychology and Selfhood in the Segregated South*. Chapel Hill: University of North Carolina Press.

Shapiro, Hugh. 1995. "The View from a Chinese Asylum: Defining Madness in 1930s Peking." PhD diss., Harvard University.

Shapiro, Hugh. 2014a. "Operatic Escapes: Performing Madness in Neuropsychiatric Beijing." In *Science and Technology in Modern China, 1880s–1940s*, edited by Jing Tsu and Benjamin Elman, 297–325. Leiden: Brill.

Shapiro, Hugh. 2014b. "Pathologizing Marriage: Neuropsychiatry and the Escape of Women in Early Twentieth-Century China." In *Psychiatry and Chinese History*, edited by Howard Chiang, 129–41. London: Pickering and Chatto.

Sulloway, Frank J. 1979. *Freud, Biologist of the Mind: Beyond the Psychoanalytic Legend*. Cambridge, MA: Harvard University Press.

Sutton, Katie. 2019. *Sex between Body and Mind: Psychoanalysis and Sexology in the German-Speaking World, 1890s–1930s*. Ann Arbor: University of Michigan Press.

Terry, Jennifer. 1999. *An American Obsession: Science, Medicine, and Homosexuality in Modern Society*. Chicago: University of Chicago Press.

Wang, Wen-Ji Wang. 2006. "'Dangxia weiren zhi daren': Dai Bingham de suren jingshen fenxi" ["This All-Important Job of Being Human at the Present": Bingham Dai's Lay Psychoanalysis]. *Xin shi xue* [*New History*] 7, no. 1: 91–142.

Zhang, Jingyuan. 1992. *Psychoanalysis in China: Literary Transformations, 1919–1949*. Ithaca, NY: East Asia Program, Cornell University.

YIDDISH SEXOLOGY

A New Language for the History of Sexuality

Zohar Weiman-Kelman

The European sciences of sex and of race, which co-emerged in the nineteenth century, cast Jewish gender—together with colonized people, women, and others—as a pathologized model of deviance. At the same time, the rising science of philology followed the same logic, deeming the Yiddish language—like the Jewish body—inferior and impure. While much has been written about the pathologizing of Jewish bodies by European sexologists (Gilman 1991; Pellegrini 1997), and while the role of Jewish scholars in the study of deviance has been recognized (Geller 2007; Bauer 2010; Biale 1997), next to nothing has been written about how European Jews theorized their own sex, in their own deviant tongue. This article proposes to rectify this lack by turning to a completely neglected body of work: sexology written in Yiddish. Turn-of-the-century Yiddish sexology offers a glimpse into diverse transnational Jewish communities who looked to the science of sex in their own language to articulate new imaginaries of corporeality and sociality. I will focus on the work of one doctor, Leonard Landis, who was by far the most prolific author of Yiddish sexology and yet remains entirely unstudied. In delving into his texts, I hope to reveal the internal complexities of Yiddish sexology at the level of language, typography, topics, influences, reach, and more. Looking outward from his work, I will argue for the vitality of including Yiddish sexology—generated at a time when so many branches of knowledge pivoted on racist fantasies of Jewish otherness—within global histories of sexuality, in order to offer a counterhistory of both race and sex.[1]

By exposing new contexts and new languages of sexuality, currently emerging studies are changing how we perceive sexology and its role in the history of sexuality. Studying Yiddish sexology not only adds to this emerging multilingual corpus of global sexology, joining the shift away from the hegemonic European center; it also complicates this shift, because Yiddish sexology was produced (in

GLQ 29:1
DOI 10.1215/10642684-10144421

part) in Europe itself, and therefore it challenges the dichotomous distinction between "the West" and its "others." Moreover, as the product of Jewish migration across the world, the transnational nature of Yiddish culture replaces the story of one-directional movement of ideas from the hegemonic center to foreign lands and marginalized people, even as it reveals multiple and complex movements within Western Europe, across Eastern Europe, and reaching to North and South America and the Middle East. Whereas many studies explore how the language of sexology reflects national processes (Mitra 2020; Chiang 2018; Fruhstuck 2003), the transnational movements of Yiddish speakers and Yiddish science also mean that Yiddish sexology does not fit into any national narrative; rather, it can reflect various national (and antinationalist) sentiments simultaneously.

The complex nature of Yiddish sexology is also evident at the level of the language, as Yiddish itself encompasses cultural and geographic multiplicity. Written in Hebrew script, Yiddish has a grammar and a vocabulary that combine German (the hegemonic language of sexology), Jewish sacred languages (Hebrew and Aramaic), Polish, Russian, English, and more (Weinreich 2008). This irreducible hybrid construction is, in fact, part of what led to the perception of the Yiddish language as inferior and bastardized (Efron 2001: 105). When we consider that Yiddish's devalued status can also be traced to the association of Yiddish with women, as *mame-loshn* (mother tongue), over and against the (masculine) Hebrew of Jewish religious scholarship (Seidman 1997) and the European vernaculars of secular Enlightenment culture (Parush 2004), it becomes all the more clear how treating the language as inferior has gone hand in hand with treating the Jewish body as deviant. Indeed, Sander Gilman (1991: 203) argues, the Jew was marked *by body and language alike.* For Yiddish-writing sexologists, the language itself was a matter of strategy, for many felt at home in their respective vernaculars and could certainly have written in those languages.[2] Therefore, choosing to study deviance in a deviant tongue can be read as a bold and indeed defiant choice.

Although there are not many works of Yiddish sexology, my research in national archives, university archives, Jewish archives, medical archives, and online archives in the United States, Europe, and the Middle East has yielded about sixty original works and works of translation dating from 1890 to 1937.[3] These works offer a window onto the particular transnational and intercultural positioning of Yiddish. Published in Warsaw, Vilnius, Riga, Berlin, Buenos Aires, Jerusalem, New York, and Los Angeles, these texts and their authors traveled across the globe. The translations span a number of languages and key thinkers: Otto Weininger, August Forel, and Max Hoddan are translated from German, Anton Nemilov is translated from Russian, W. Flatau is translated from Polish, and Margret Sanger is translated from English, for example. The original Yiddish works also tend to rely heavily on non-Yiddish thinkers, citing Richard von Krafft-Ebing, Havelock Ellis, and Magnus Hirschfeld, among others. Yiddish sexology touches upon the same range of issues occupying sexology in other tongues: marital advice (*Man un froy* [*Husband and wife*]), impotence (*Der haleber mensh* [*The half man*]), masturbation (*Zind gegen di natur* [*Sins against nature*]), and deviance (*Di libe* [*Love*]), to take four examples written by the aforementioned Dr. Leonard Landis and published in New York approximately between 1900 and 1910 (none of his works bear a date of publication).

Landis was born in Iasi, Romania, in 1870. He graduated from the Medical College at New York University in 1892 and is included in the 1903 album *New York University: Its History, Influence, Equipment and Characteristics, with Biographical Sketches and Portraits of Founders, Benefactors, Officers and Alumni.* Beyond this record, his many claims to fame in both Europe and the United States seem suspect, though they do convey the stage on which he imagined himself to be standing. For example, Landis claims that while working in Europe in 1893 he published his "famous article" about cholera, which caused a "worldwide stir because in it I proved that Cholera derives from the water one drinks" (*Mener fraynd*: 115). He goes on to blame the "fanatic Mohamadins" (115) for bringing the disease from the pilgrimage to Mecca, revealing that Jewish sexology was not at all free of racist conceptions, even those specifically mirroring the worst anti-Semitic narratives that accused the Jews of spreading plagues since the Middle Ages. I have not found any such scientific article nor have I found any citations leading to Landis.

If Landis did not actually bring his science of sex into the global field of sexology (despite his claims of working in London, Vienna, and Berlin in addition to New York), he did take on the role of bringing this science to his Yiddish-speaking audience. Landis (*Di libe*: 5) introduces his book *Love* this way: "Poets have only sung of love, novel writers described it. The medical science however, has researched it, and these studies of the newest science will be explained in the following chapters of this book, *Di libe.*" Under the rubric of "love" Landis fits an especially wide range of topics, most of which we might more readily associate with sex. He compares feelings of love between men and women, quoting diverse sources ranging from folk sayings to "ancient doctors" who claim that, contrary to popular opinion, women have stronger "love urges" than men (24). In the chapter titled "The woman-man and the man-woman," he defines the masculine woman as "one of the strangest mysteries of love" (18). The chapters "Love and smell" and "Love and beauty" (the latter of which actually focuses on the sense of sight) explore physical conditions of sexual attraction. He also tackles mating rituals in the plant and animal kingdom, for example, "time for love among the salmon," who have, like all fish, "the weakest love feelings of all the animals" (110). Overall, the vision of love/sex Landis offers is heteronormative, reproductive, and monogamous.

In his book *Di hayrat* (*Marriage*) Landis says sex should not be too frequent (69), should be "complete" (70), and should be free of contraception other than avoiding intercourse altogether (74). In *Di oysgelasene velt* (*The Licentious World*) Landis lists the detrimental circumstances facing men in his current day and age: women's fashion, modern dance styles, and young people bathing together, as well as the high population density in factories and tenement buildings. The result of these circumstances is "the existence of brothels at best, and at its most problematic, rape" (69). Regarding prostitution, Landis takes a particularly progressive approach, writing that women "should ask themselves whether they think being with one man for his money is better than being with many men also for money" (69). Still, he concludes that prostitution has many bad consequences, such as venereal diseases. He then turns to the reader, saying if he suspects that he has been infected, he should seek treatment in Landis's clinic (70). Landis thus positions his sexology as offering both theoretical and practical assistance.

As part of the task of "explaining the newest research," Landis takes on the role of mediating hegemonic sexology and its many thinkers to his Yiddish-speaking audience. As mediator, Landis recruits the authority of the most famous sexologists. At times he does so by invoking the broad category of unnamed *gelernte* (learned scholars). Other times he names particular scholars as sources, such as Richard von Krafft-Ebing, Cesare Lombroso, Friedrich Salomon Krauss, Havelock Ellis, and many more. The most scientific form of reference Landis employs is providing citations in parentheses, including author names or book titles (never both!), sometimes with page numbers. However, careful work to trace his sources and citations proves revealing, if not damning. Not only does he consistently miscite and misspell sources (rendering some sources untraceable), he also freely plagiarizes the work of others. Sometimes he does this to reproduce their findings (as was indeed a norm of the time); occasionally he completely upends their original positions. This license implies that Landis did not expect that other authors would arrive at his Yiddish writings or that his readership would read beyond his own work.

Positioning himself as an exclusive source allows Landis to engage with key texts of sexology while mitigating some of their anti-Semitic reverberations by circumventing the less hospitable aspects. For example, in the work *Mener fraynd* (*Friend of Man*), in which Landis leans heavily on the work of Krafft-Ebing, Landis removes references to phrenology, omitting all skull measurements and their consequent diagnoses, though these held a prominent place in Krafft-Ebing's cases and in other sources from which Landis drew (such as Charcot's *Archives de neurologie*). This omission is not surprising considering phrenology's key role at the intersection of the science of race and sex, locating racial difference on the body, though not necessarily focused on the Jewish body (Greenblatt 1995). Landis also offers his own engagement with the racist debates distinguishing male and female bodies, which claimed that racialized bodies undermine said distinctions and should therefore be read as deviant. Such racist projects deemed African women overly masculine based on clitoral measurements (Somerville 2000) and Jewish men overly feminine based on the act of circumcision (Gilman 1991). Landis does dedicate multiple chapters across his oeuvre to the question of circumcision, but rather than addressing anti-Semitic claims directly, he cites circumcision as a modern health practice. For example, in *Der tayvel* (*The Devil*), a book dedicated to syphilis, Landis warns his readers about oral sex, deeming the act "barbaric," and suggests circumcision and maintaining a high level of personal hygiene as effective means of prevention (62–63). Landis thus addresses anti-Semitic claims without explicitly entering into dialogue with them. Perhaps in writing for a Yiddish-speaking audience, who was therefore presumably predominantly if not entirely Jewish, he did not feel the need to answer sexology's racist claims directly.

What Landis offers should thus be read as internal Jewish discourse, though his references to Jewish bodies, life, and sources are surprisingly sparse and do not offer a monolithic position. For example, in his book *Zind gegen di natur* (*Sins against Nature*), dedicated primarily to masturbation, Landis aligns Jews with other races, writing that "umnatirlekhe mentshlekhe farbindung" (unnatural human interactions) as well as "zelbst-bafridikung" (self-satisfaction) are common everywhere, as well as among Jews (99). He mentions that the Torah and the Talmud (the latter of which is the central postbiblical rabbinic text) condemn homosexual relations, but shortly afterward he abandons the discussion of Jewish history and tradition and instead elaborates on the prevalence of sex with animals among many non-Jewish ethnic groups. In the same book, Landis expresses explicit criticism of the Jewish way of life in the chapter "Der vide fun a Yeshive-bokher" ("The confession of a Yeshiva boy," referring to the traditional all-male setting dedicated to Jewish scholarship), where he blames the yeshiva for "emphasizing mind while destroying the body" (33). Though Landis characterizes his patient as pale, weak, and effeminate, very much in line with anti-Semitic depictions of Jewish masculinity, instead of attributing these features to the student's race Landis names them as symptoms of masturbation. Interestingly, though

Figure 1. Title page from *Zind gegen di natur* (*Sins against Nature*).
YIVO Archives, New York.

here masturbation is described as a group activity, Landis does not make any reference to homosexuality and seems to take for granted the homosocial nature of the religious setting.

Despite criticizing the Jewish system of learning, one of the most distinguishing factors of Landis's texts, besides being in Yiddish, is the layout of their title page, which is modeled upon sacred Jewish texts (fig. 1). We might consider this a form of visual camouflage disguising the actual genre of the book and perhaps making the scientific content more accessible to an audience more accustomed to reading sacred books. This camouflage would not be limited to just the graphic elements of the decorative frame containing the book's title, *Sins against nature*, and the triangular layout beneath it. Landis also uses a biblical verse as an epigraph under the frame: "The glory of young men is their strength," from Proverbs 20:29 (though he miscites it as verse 28). The quote appears first in Hebrew, as this is the language in which the sacred Jewish texts Landis is mimicking were written, alongside a Yiddish translation of the line. The triangular typesetting is also misleading, for instead of containing religious words of wisdom, here it contains highlights of Landis's career: former assistant at the University Dispensary, Delmit Dispensary, Post Graduate Hospital, Folk Clinic, Bellevue Hospital Dispensary, Lebanon Hospital, New York Oral Institute, New York Infirmary, German Folk Clinic, Mount Sinai Hospital Dispensary, and former doctor of the Panama Railroad Company. The lines of text beneath the triangle specify that Landis is the director of the New York Electrical Medicine Institute (to which I have found no further reference) and mention books he's authored and the health journal he publishes. The only elements in English are his address and office hours and the price of twenty cents, which could be the price of the book or the price of a visit to his office. Also worth noting is that here, as in the rest of his works, Landis uses a heavily Germanized Yiddish, evident both in word choice and spelling, as was common in much of early Yiddish science, as well as other genres of literature, which attempted to gain respectability by imitating German. However, the juxtaposition of the Germanized language and the gestures to religious textuality stand out as a particularly unusual combination.

This juxtaposition is also evident on the level of content, for example in *Di libe* (*Love*), in the chapter dedicated to sadomasochism (see fig. 2). The chapter deals in the psychopathology of the encounter of "love and pain," telling the life stories of Sacher von Masoch and the Marquis de Sade, and offering sensational case studies of historical and contemporary mass murders connected to crimes of passion. This chapter, alongside others in the same book, seems to rely heavily on the work of British sexologist Havelock Ellis, namely in the section "Love and

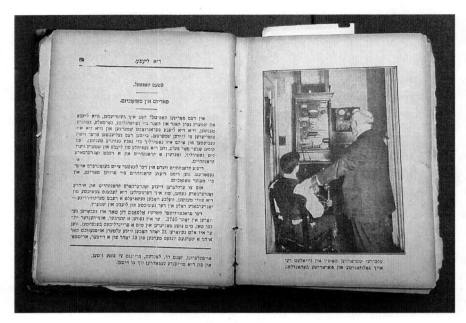

Figure 2. First page of the chapter "Sadism and Masochism" from *Di libe*, accompanied by an image identified as an x-ray machine. YIVO Archives, New York.

Pain" from volume 3 of his *Studies in the Psychology of Sex*, originally published in 1903 (Ellis 2004). While it is beyond the scope of this article to explore the fascinating dynamic of plagiarism, translations, and interpretation at work here, I will simply quote Landis's own summary of his positioning vis-à-vis dominant sexological discourse. He writes:

> Learned men like Krafft-Ebing, Schrenck, Eulenburg and Féré [all quoted in Ellis, who is not mentioned in this list!] have made the biggest effort to study this unusual, antinatural [distinctly not the word for unnatural] phenomenon of sadism and masochism, which is only another form of love and pain. One suffers all manner of pain from the woman one loves, purely out of love. The woman allows herself to be offended and humiliated. (*Di libe*: 61)

Landis here recasts pain as something one might be willing to suffer for the sake of love, entirely missing or actively negating the potential pleasure of pain so central to the discussion of sadism and masochism that he himself invokes by naming prominent scholars, all of whom are quoted in Ellis's chapter. The fact that Ellis himself is not named in this list only underscores his role as a main (and thus invisible) source (much like the way Krafft-Ebing disappears from the chapters relying most heavily on his work).

At the same time, the chapter invokes two additional discourses absent from Ellis: the discourse of medical technology, and Jewish religious discourse. The technological aspect is evident from the photograph on the right in Figure 2, which Landis titles "X-ray machine and violet ray and Galvanic and Faradic treatment." How the treatment actually works remains unspecified throughout his work, though it is clearly in line with the zeitgeist, when various electrotherapeutic treatments were being developed and refuted (Wexler 2017). The religious text with which Landis ends his chapter is from the Talmud (in the Hebrew original rather than in Yiddish): "He who wishes to take a wife should check her brothers." While Landis explains how this background check can save you from marrying a mass murderer, the religious wisdom seems at best tangentially connected to the topic of sadomasochism and seems especially distant from the X-ray machine the chapter began with. If the technological discourse positions Landis on the border between cutting-edge medicine and quackery in turn-of-the-century New York, the invocation of Jewish religious text positions him on the border between rural Eastern European Jewry and urban immigrant life, where one no longer knows "what's cooking in every pot" (*Di libe*: 63). The combination of multiple discourses is not unusual for Yiddish sexology; nor does it stand out in other sexological discourses that were intimately linked to the medical, legal, and religious discourses of their time (Spector 2016). Still, what stands out is the polyvocality of the text, in the tensions between the mundane and the pathological, the religious and the sexological. Rather than addressing these tensions as such, by orchestrating them according to his own agenda, Landis positions himself as narrator of and authority over the multiple bodies of knowledge. Reading across Landis's work, it appears he is recruiting the science of sex at large while, to a large extent, manipulating and even misinterpreting it. Similarly, he recruits Jewish textual norms and religious law to bolster his own agenda, gain legitimacy within the Jewish community, and exercise authority.

This authority was indeed challenged over the years, as is evident from ubiquitous references in the American press, both in Yiddish and English, to legal scandals Landis was implicated in, culminating in the revocation of his medical license in 1927 (*New York Times* n.d.). Shortly afterward, on February 25, 1927, *Forverts* (*Forward*), a major Yiddish newspaper, published a piece titled "Finally Rid of the Faker Dr. Landis" (*Forverts* [*Forward*] 1927). The article recounts the fortune Landis supposedly made by "terrifying patients" and accuses him of merciless advertising—first with signs that "were inescapable on the East side twenty years ago," and then with his books, which he used to give out for free and then began to sell at rising prices—and of extorting funds (mainly by forcing patients to use his new and revolutionary X-ray machine). Finally, and not surprisingly, the article also accuses Landis of obscenity for having his very own "Museum of the Human Body," which displayed "frankly and freely in which forms sexual diseases come" by way of wax sculptures (though it is not clear from the Yiddish if the sculptures depict the diseases or the acts that lead to them).[4]

This article and many others that appeared in the American press aligned Landis's science with the tradition of so-called quackery rather than the field of modern medicine to which he aspired to belong. Indeed, the only reference to Landis in contemporary studies of American history of medicine are in Alan Kraut's chapter "'There Could Also Be Magic in Barbarian Medicin': American Nurses, Physicians, and Quacks" (Kraut 1995). There Kraut writes of a 1921 Cleveland Health survey report bemoaning "quacks" advertising medical services to immigrant groups. The report refers to "the same quack [Landis]" writing ads in several papers calling to "my Rumanian brothers" or to my "sick Lithuanian brothers" or even "sick Italians, don't be discouraged. Thousands of your countrymen have found health and happiness by going to see Dr. Landis" (Kraut 1995: 220). Often the ads stressed the advantage of a doctor who shared your tongue. The Landis of this 1921 report, writes Kraut, is the same Landis who was prosecuted in New York state by the Bureau of Industries and Immigration in 1915 and given a jail sentence of thirty days and a fine of one hundred dollars for placing such advertisements (334n88). As Christine Ford Chapin (2020: 4) explains, the American Medical Association "sought to place medical practice outside the commercial sphere, which they deemed plebian and crass. Thus, the AMA ethical code forbade blatant competition among physicians. Prohibited activities included speaking ill of another doctor, openly advertising, or even posting an office sign with service prices." While it is clear that Landis breached many of these codes, in his 1924 English-language book *The Physician and His People* he preemptively addresses the precise claims raised against him in his time (and afterward) by writing: "Instead of slinking in hidden paths and by backdoors, I spoke openly and directly. Is that faking? Judge for yourself who is the faker and who is the honourable doctor" (329).

A century later, how are we to judge Landis's sexological contribution? Hardly a proper object for any history, he epitomizes the deviance of Yiddish and sexology themselves, both as objects and as methods. And still, recovering this body of work and Yiddish sexology at large must be recognized as a rare opportunity to encounter "living, breathing [Yiddish] speaking inverts and perverts," to echo Gayle Rubin's formulation (Butler 1994: 80), offering a vital counterhistory to the Jew as object of study, and to the Jew as participant in hegemonic sexology. Indeed, at the same time as the Jewish body was singled out for its difference and deviance, as the science of sex developed into the twentieth century, some European Jewish men were positioned in such a way to enable them to transition from the objects of science to its producers, alongside but far surpassing women, some of them Jewish (Leng 2018), joining and leading key debates within sexology. Jews came to play a key role in the consolidation of the discipline of *Sexualwissenschaft* (as Iwan Bloch termed the science of sex in 1906). With the rise of the Third Reich, the Nazis attacked sexology for being both a degenerate science and specifically a "Jewish science" (Haeberle 1982: 307). Accordingly, Haeberle marks the Second World War as a tragic rupture for the discipline and calls for a recovery of the past of sexology: "If we do not regain our past that has been stolen from us, we sexologists will not have the academic future to which we are otherwise well entitled" (321). And still, even in Haeberle's comprehensive recovery project (culminating in the Haeberle-Hirschfeld Archive of Sexology at Humboldt University in Berlin), there is no record of Yiddish sexology. Taking the complex history of Jews and sexology into account, the stakes of the recovery of Yiddish sexology are crystallized: a lost body of work as well as an avenue of access to encountering and theorizing the Jewish body, over and against forces that sought not only to pathologize it but also to eradicate it.

Today the only remaining major Yiddish-speaking community is located in Jewish ultra-Orthodox circles (Shandler 2006), and the very fact that Yiddish sexology even exists comes as a surprise to many. Indeed, the radical imaginaries of the Yiddish sexologists are all but lost in a world where Yiddish is associated only with conservative religiosity, rendering so much of the Yiddish past unknown and unstudied. Instead of conservative religiosity, in returning to these materials we encounter a double transgression, as Yiddish sexologists pushed both the boundaries of Jewish society by embracing scientific sexology and the boundaries of sexology by adhering to the Yiddish language, thereby producing their own version of (Jewish) modernity. This Yiddish version of modernity was erased not just by the Nazi extermination project but also by Stalinism, Zionism, and the more gradual process of assimilation. As Yiddish sexology came to a halt, Jews began to produce Hebrew sexology in pre-state Palestine, bolstering the rise of Jewish nationalism and the pathologizing of Arab bodies, specifically the Arab-Jewish bodies of Mizrahi Jews (of Middle Eastern and North African descent) (Hirsch 2009; Kozma 2010). Recovering Yiddish sexology thus offers not only a history that has been erased but also a glimpse into what *could have been* had Jewish history unfolded differently, revealing radical imaginaries of potential Jewish futures beyond heteronormativity and nationalism.

Notes

I am grateful for the research assistance of Shiri Shapira and Shira Levy, for the insightful reading of Durba Mitra and Marty Fink, and for the rigorous feedback from the anonymous reviewers and the special issue editors.

1. I use counterhistory in opposition "not only to dominant narratives, but also to prevailing modes of historical thought and methods of research," following Saidiya Hartman (2008), who relies on Catherine Gallagher and Stephen Greenblatt.
2. For further reading on Jewish languages and Jewish multilingualism, see Miller and Norich 2016.
3. While a sparse amount of Yiddish writing pertaining to sex has been produced for ultra-Orthodox audiences, this work positions itself outside of the scientific field of sexology and is therefore beyond the scope of my project. Similarly, I do not include religious tractates pertaining to sex that existed from the end of the eighteenth century (though these were more likely overall to be written in Hebrew).
4. Incidentally, in a 1912 English-language pamphlet titled *The Tree of Knowledge*, Landis (1912) mentions an identical "life-like wax figure display" of venereal disease in the Sexual and Hygienic Exhibit in Dresden in 1911. "Unfortunately, such an exhibition in this country would be entirely impossible," he writes, "due to the well-meaning but narrow-minded puritanical influences."

References

Bauer, Heike. 2010. "'Race,' Normativity and the History of Sexuality: Magnus Hirschfeld's Racism and the Early-Twentieth-Century Sexology." *Psychology and Sexuality* 1, no. 3: 239–49. https://doi.org/10.1080/19419899.2010.494899.

Biale, David. 1997. "The Discipline of *Sexualwissenschaft* Emerges in Germany, Creating Divergent Notions of European Jewry." In *Yale Companion to Jewish Writing and Thought in German Culture, 1096–1996*, edited by Jack Zipes, 273–79. New Haven, CT: Yale University Press.

Butler, Judith. 1994. "Sexual Traffic." *Differences: A Journal of Feminist Cultural Studies* 6, nos. 2–3: 62–100.

Chapin, Christine Ford. 2020. "Health Policy." *The Oxford Handbook of American Political History*. April. https://doi.org/10.1093/oxfordhb/9780199341788.013.33.

Chiang, Howard. 2018. *After Eunuchs: Science, Medicine, and the Transformation of Sex in Modern China*. New York: Columbia University Press.

Efron, John M. 2001. *Medicine and the German Jews: A History*. New Haven, CT: Yale University Press.

Ellis, Havelock. 2004. *Studies in the Psychology of Sex, Volume 3: Analysis of the Sexual Impulse; Love and Pain; The Sexual Impulse in Women*. https://www.gutenberg.org/ebooks/13612.

Forverts (*Forward*). 1927. "Finally Rid of the Faker Dr. Landis." February 25.

Fruhstuck, Sabine. 2003. *Colonizing Sex: Sexology and Social Control in Modern Japan*. Berkeley: University of California Press.

Geller, Jay. 2007. *On Freud's Jewish Body: Mitigating Circumcisions*. New York: Fordham University Press.

Gilman, Sander L. 1991. *The Jew's Body*. New York: Routledge.

Greenblatt, S. H. 1995. "Phrenology in the Science and Culture of the 19th Century." *Neurosurgery* 37, no. 4: 790–804; discussion 804–5. https://doi.org/10.1227/00006123–99510000–00025.

Haeberle, Erwin J. 1982. "The Jewish Contribution to the Development of Sexology." *Journal of Sex Research* 18, no. 4: 305–23.

Hartman, Saidiya. 2008. "Venus in Two Acts." *Small Axe* 12, no. 2: 1–14.

Hirsch, Dafna. 2009. "Zionist Eugenics, Mixed Marriage, and the Creation of a 'New Jewish Type.'" *Journal of the Royal Anthropological Institute* 15, no. 3: 592–609.

Kozma, Liat. 2010. "Sexology in the Yishuv: The Rise and Decline of Sexual Consultation in Tel Aviv, 1930–39." *International Journal of Middle East Studies* 42, no. 2: 231–49.

Kraut, Alan M. 1995. *Silent Travelers: Germs, Genes, and the Immigrant Menace*. Baltimore, MD: Johns Hopkins University Press.

Landis, Leonard. 1912. *The Tree of Life*. Self-published.

Landis, Leonard. 1924. *The Physician and His People*. New York: American Association of Independent Physicians.

Landis, Leonard. n.d. *Der tayvel* (*The Devil*). Self-published.

Landis, Leonard. n.d. *Di hayrat* (*Marriage*). Self-published.

Landis, Leonard. n.d. *Di libe* (*Love*). Self-published.

Landis, Leonard. n.d. *Di oysgelasene velt* (*The Licentious World*). Self-published.

Landis, Leonard. n.d. *Mener fraynd* (*Friend of Man*). Self-published.

Landis, Leonard. n.d. *Zind gegen di natur* (*Sins against Nature*). Self-published.

Leng, Kirsten. 2018. *Sexual Politics and Feminist Science: Women Sexologists in Germany, 1900–1933*. Ithaca, NY: Cornell University Press. http://www.jstor.org/stable/10.7591/j.ctt1wlvjsc.

Miller, Joshua L., and Anita Norich, eds. 2016. *Languages of Modern Jewish Cultures:*

Comparative Perspectives. Ann Arbor: University of Michigan Press. https://doi.org
/10.3998/mpub.8824672.

Mitra, Durba. 2020. *Indian Sex Life: Sexuality and the Colonial Origins of Modern
Social Thought*. Princeton, NJ: Princeton University Press. https://doi.org/10.2307
/j.ctvkjb4fc.

New York Times. 1927. "Dr. Landis's License Revoked by Regents; Head of the House of
Health Declared Guilty of Fraud and Deceit." February 24.

Parush, Iris. 2004. *Reading Jewish Women: Marginality and Modernization in
Nineteenth-Century Eastern European Jewish Society*. Waltham, MA: Brandeis University Press.

Pellegrini, Ann. 1997. *Performance Anxieties: Staging Psychoanalysis, Staging Race*.
New York: Routledge.

Seidman, Naomi. 1997. *A Marriage Made in Heaven: The Sexual Politics of Hebrew and
Yiddish*. Berkeley: University of California Press.

Shandler, Jeffrey. 2006. *Adventures in Yiddishland: Postvernacular Language and
Culture*. Berkeley: University of California Press. http://www.loc.gov/catdir/toc
/ecip058/2005005293.html.

Somerville, Siobhan B. 2000. *Queering the Color Line: Race and the Invention of Homosexuality in American Culture*. Durham, NC: Duke University Press.

Spector, Scott. 2016. *Violent Sensations: Sex, Crime, and Utopia in Vienna and Berlin,
1860–1914*. Chicago: University of Chicago Press.

Weinreich, Max. 2008. *History of the Yiddish Language*. New Haven, CT: Yale University
Press.

Wexler, Anna. 2017. "Medical Battery in the United States (1870–1920): Electrotherapy
at Home and in the Clinic." *Journal of the History of Medicine and Allied Sciences*
72, no. 2: 166–92.

TAXONOMICALLY QUEER?

Sexology and New Queer, Trans, and Asexual Identities

Kadji Amin

Something has shifted in vernacular discourses about gender and sexuality in the global North, something that queer theory has not caught up to and that departs discomfitingly from the values and critical habits of queer and trans theorization. In 1990, Judith Butler (1990: xxx) could still take a "heterosexual matrix," in which binary gender and heterosexuality followed ineluctably from bodily sex, as the object of her deconstructive critique. Likewise, in 1990, Eve Sedgwick (1990: 22) could still make this comment about her first axiom, "People are different from each other": "It is astonishing how few respectable conceptual tools we have for dealing with this self-evident fact. A tiny number of inconceivably coarse axes of categorization have been painstakingly inscribed in current critical and political thought: gender, race, class, nationality, sexual orientation are pretty much the available distinctions." As I write this in 2021, Butler's heterosexual matrix has exploded in a way hitherto unimaginable. Vernacular discourses have subdivided the "tiny number of inconceivably coarse axes" of gender and sexual orientation to which Sedgwick refers into a series of more precise distinctions. If the heterosexual matrix was a tight and immobile structure, then the contemporary system to which I refer works more like a kaleidoscope, in which each axis of definition is mobile and may be combined with any other axis, making way for an almost infinite array of variations.

The contemporary moment is the result of decades of intracommunity, subcultural, and online debates. These debates have led to the dissemination—in university safe space and trans 101 trainings, in the Asexual Visibility and Education Network's well-maintained website, and in Facebook's drop-down menu of seventy-one gender options, to name just a few key sites—of a new, vernacular system of classification. This vernacular system takes as its starting point the truism within contemporary queer and trans cultures that "gender is who you go to bed *as*, and

GLQ 29:1

DOI 10.1215/10642684-10144435

© 2023 by Duke University Press

sexuality is who you want to go to bed *with*," generating from this foundational distinction a proliferation of genders and sexualities. Gender and sexuality, moreover, are no longer the only two axes of categorization. Gender is now widely understood to include the three axes of assigned gender, gender identity, and gender expression. For asexual thinkers, sexual orientation is merely one variety of orientation, along with romantic, sensual, and aesthetic orientation. For many, particularly younger people, this system represents the cutting edge. It embodies utopian hopes for a world in which no one's gender, sexuality, or mode of attraction would be presumed in advance and in which everyone would have recourse to a nuanced and nimble vocabulary through which to know, define, and communicate their own unique gender and sexual subjectivity. In this utopian imaginary—which I call *combinatorial queerness*—sexual, gender, and relational liberation take place through a multiplying menu of increasingly fine-grained identity options.

This utopian imaginary is founded on the method of taxonomy. But what could be further from the *queer*—which might be glossed as a deconstructive method of troubling categorizations—than taxonomy, a scientific method of establishing them? Similarly, trans studies has defined prefixial trans-, trans*, and the transing as dynamic movements that traverse, precede, or exceed fixed categorizations (Stryker, Currah, and Moore 2008; Hayward and Weinstein 2015). Yet if queer and trans studies are to remain even nominally beholden to the peoples and cultures from which these fields borrow their names and to whom they at times purport to do justice, these fields must contend with the taxonomical ideals of contemporary queer, trans, and asexual culture. (In what follows, I reference these cultures with the shorthand umbrella term *queer*, partially in order to make tangible their dissonance with queer theoretical ideals.)

This article argues that contemporary queer culture in the global North is in the midst of a taxonomical renaissance. The will to birth and affirm quasi-infinite combinatorial possibilities of being by recombining the mobile axes of gender, sexual, and relational subjectivity is the widely shared value that animates this taxonomical renaissance. This article examines the untimely echoes between these contemporary vernacular knowledges and German sexologist Magnus Hirschfeld's early twentieth-century taxonomy of sexual intermediaries, which forwards a combinatorially lush kaleidoscope of sexed possibilities that outflanks even contemporary developments. By way of this juxtaposition, I conclude that contemporary queer systems of identity are the latest iteration of the classificatory logics behind sexology in particular and racial science more generally. This article mines the tensions between queer and trans theory's hostility to sexology and the apotheosis of sexological logics within contemporary queer culture. In so doing, it plumbs a key methodological question: How are the scholarly fields of queer and trans studies—which have taken shape in ambivalent resistance to sexology and taxonomy alike—to contend with the departure of the cultures to which they owe their existence from this basic orientation? My goal is neither to unequivocally excoriate contemporary queer taxonomies nor to celebrate their creative and world-making possibilities. Instead, I propose that it is time for a reckoning with the foundational role of sexological thinking in contemporary queer culture. I seek to begin a conversation, both among scholars and within queer communities, about the consequences and possibilities of this inheritance.

The Renaissance of Taxonomy

"Gender and sexuality are separate" is an oft-repeated maxim within contemporary queer culture, as well as the opening gambit of any trans 101 or university safe space training. This maxim asserts not only an analytic (and perhaps even ontological) distinction, but also a combinatorial proposition: any gender identity may occur in any combination with any sexual orientation. I am implicated within this understanding, which was vital to the evolution of my own queer and then trans subjectivity during the first decade of the 2000s. Had gender not been separate and distinct from sexuality, I would not have been able to claim a trans fag identity, a position then newly viable, that contravened the expectation that masculinity on a female-assigned body went hand in hand with attraction to women and femininity—let's call that the "butch" model. Whereas the butch model (in which gender and sexuality are coimplicated) has deep historical and even cross-cultural resonance, the trans fag model (in which gender and sexuality are distinct), of which I am a product, has only recently achieved widespread legibility in a few locations in the global North. I offer this preamble to implicate myself in the historical transformations I discuss here as well as to demonstrate the subject-forming capacities of basic taxonomical principles. I am fully cognizant, however, of the fact that, from Magnus Hirschfeld's early twentieth-century effort to distinguish transvestites from homosexuals to John Money's invention of the concept of gender as a means of disciplining the racialized plasticity of sexed bodies (Gill-Peterson 2018), the distinction between gender and sexuality was always *a sexological invention*—a taxonomical principle masquerading as an ontological distinction. Worse, as I will elaborate shortly, sexological taxonomies are implicated within white supremacy. This is to say that my identity, like that of many queer- and trans-identified people of color, is a sexological and white supremacist aftereffect.

Even as I was exploring the possibilities of the separation of gender and sexuality during the 2000s, vernacular taxonomies of gender identity, gender expression, sexual orientation, and romantic orientation were proliferating beyond my own purview in public and semipublic spheres outside of the jurisdiction of medical professionals. Today, the largely invisible intracommunity work of coining new terminologies and debating the merits of new forms of categorization during the 2000s–2010s has gone mainstream. These newer identities (with the notable exception of transgender) cannot be said to be institutionalized in any traditional sense: they do not correspond to risk groups, scholarly fields, or dedicated lines of funding. With the exception of *transgender* and *asexual*, they are not even attempting to dialogue with medicine or law. However, the internet, social media apps, and university trainings are proving to be effective centers for dissemination. As I write this, these vernacular taxonomies are among the most visible and well-known artifacts of contemporary queer culture; many university students arrive in the queer and trans studies classroom already fluent in them. If, during the late nineteenth and early twentieth centuries, some white, middle-class people would realize they were homosexuals (or inverts, or contrary-sexuals) by reading a specialized medical textbook, now a more democratically diverse array of people might realize they are nonbinary (or aromantic, or pansexual) by discovering the term in a drop-down menu or meme.

Part of what has enabled this plethora of new identities to break into mainstream visibility is the fact that they are presented according to the familiar and eminently rational conventions of taxonomical thinking. The popular production, often by ordinary internet users, of graphs and trees ranging from simple to quite complex that visually represent the relations between new identities according to the taxonomic principle of rank attest to a popular hunger for taxonomic forms of representation and reasoning.[1] In some cases, the architecture of taxonomy serves to contain and safely domesticate the unruly and disruptive potential of terms that might otherwise deconstruct the basis of the entire category in which they are housed. For instance, if *asexuality* were not reassuringly categorized as merely one among a number of "types" of sexual orientation, it might explode the conceptual and ontological foundations of sexuality itself. *Asexuality* thus conceived could name a vector of escape from the network of power that produces then ferrets out sexuality as the hidden and mysterious, yet explanatory and causal core of modern selfhood (Foucault [1976] 1990).[2] Similarly, *gender fluid*, *nonbinary*, and *agender* have been inhabited as radical critiques, not only of the limited imagination that only allows for two genders, but more consequentially of the biopolitical construction of gender itself as a fixed, innate identity possessed by each individual. Using the taxonomical method to categorize gender fluid, nonbinary, and agender *with* other gender identities, or to claim asexuality as a legitimate sexual orientation *like* homosexuality or heterosexuality, is not just paradoxical; it also contains these modes of being securely *within* the sexological system of compulsory gender and sexuality they might otherwise be deployed *against*.

The Trouble with Taxonomy

This is only the tip of the iceberg when it comes to taxonomy's profoundly conservative history. The problem is not only that the available taxonomies have been crude and coarse, as Sedgwick suggests, or that taxonomies are fixed and restrictive whereas gender and sexuality are idiosyncratic and fluid. The deeper issue is that, as a body of new scholarship is critically exploring, taxonomy is a scientific method that was developed in and through its colonial, anti-Black, and pathologizing uses. The longtime queer and trans scholarly suspicion of taxonomy stems most directly from its usage by nineteenth- and early twentieth-century sexologists to classify and pathologize a proliferating array of forms of sexual and gendered deviance. As damaging as sexological taxonomies have been for many gender and sexual deviants, to be sexologically diagnosable in the first place was *a white distinction*—a testament to the individuality, complexity, and value of white bodies and psyches. As many scholars have demonstrated, Indigenous and racialized peoples were not considered deviant as sexological individuals who might *be* homosexuals, sadists, sexual fetishists, etc., but rather en masse, as constitutively and polymorphously perverse populations (Ross 2005; Driskill 2016). This leads Keguro Macharia (2020: 563–64) to pointedly write, "African queerness—the queerness of the savage—is *not related* to the taxonomic-sexological marking of gay, lesbian, bisexual, trans*, intersex, and the proliferation of conditions and practices described by Richard von Krafft-Ebing." The upstart science of sexology claimed legitimacy by promising to address the threat white sexual deviants posed to eugenic breeding and to white claims to the civilizational distinction of binary sex (Stein 2015).

Beyond the domain of sexology proper, anti-Blackness was foundational to the taxonomical project of generating racial and species hierarchies and thus to the development of empirical science itself. As Zakiyyah Iman Jackson (2020: 173) writes, "The pursuit of an observable and comparative basis of racial taxonomy and typology is central to the rise of empirical science, an organizing principle, not a matter merely incidental to it." Colonial conquest and expansion were likewise materially and conceptually crucial to the scientific project of taxonomy. Greta LaFleur (2018: 141) characterizes the eighteenth-century taxonomical project of botanical science as based on "colonial prospecting"—the search, through colonial expansion, for new specimens that would test the validity of existing schemas of classification. Finally, the universalist truth effect of taxonomy was crucial to the project of advancing European epistemologies as the only ones with the status of ontological truth, a project that required either delegitimizing the cosmologies of the Indigenous and the colonized, or translating them into commensurate terms (Mitra 2020). In short, taxonomy was a key method by which European science objectified the world, rendering it assimilable to European schemas that justified settler/colonial projects of enslavement, land theft, and rule.

Queer Taxonomy?

In light of this noxious history, is it even conceivable to put a queer spin on taxonomy? This question dovetails with methodological debates in queer studies that ask if scientific and social scientific methods that have been part of the objectification of the world in ways organized around anti-Blackness, colonial conquest, and the pathologization of deviance can be repurposed for more innocent or even progressive ends or whether such methods inevitably perpetuate the hierarchical, violent, and racist epistemological frameworks from which they emerged (Love 2015; Ghaziani and Brim 2019). We might locate the contemporary queer, trans, and asexual taxonomical renaissance as a crucial case study within this debate.

Arguably, the new queer classification system recontextualizes and repurposes the taxonomical method for queer ends. Strikingly, these new taxonomies emerge *from below*—they are vernacular in origin and fundamentally undo the doctor/patient, scientist/specimen, and confession/interpretation hierarchy that has been the foundation of scientific taxonomies. One might posit that it is this hierarchy of power, not the taxonomic method itself, that has enabled taxonomy to be used to such epistemologically violent ends. Furthermore, these new taxonomies are distinguished by the ethos of self-identification. While a range of blogs, videos, and memes engage in the project of defining each new term and classificatory principle, they simultaneously urge users to take up the terms in their own ways and ascribe their own meanings to them. According to the collective identity model of asexuality, for instance, "an asexual person is anyone who uses the term 'asexual' to describe themselves. The label can only be applied internally, no one has the power to create a set of criteria which determine who 'is' and 'is not' asexual" (Collective Identity Model). This is a classification system that is willing to renounce true systematicity in favor of idiosyncratic individual interpretations because, strictly speaking, each term could mean practically anything. Since these taxonomies were generated through a community discussion that remains ongoing, the system itself remains mobile and open to continuous change from below. This might include the further multiplication of existing taxons and even the redefinition of the principal axes of categorization.

Most significantly, the intent of this taxonomical system runs counter to that of typical scientific taxonomies. For instance, in biological taxonomies of species, which originate in Carl Linnaeus's *Systema Naturae*, locating a specimen means classing it within a hierarchy of ranks, each of which informs us of its key (in this case, morphological) characteristics, from the most general to the most specific. The aim of new queer taxonomies, by contrast, is not to locate and fix an individual within a hierarchical pyramid or tree, but rather to put the key axes—gender, sexual, romantic, and relational orientation—*into motion* in order to capacitate a nearly infinite range of combinations, and thereby, forms of personhood. Basic to the general validity of species taxonomies is the claim that *these* principles for the classification of life are the most universal, economical, and significant—they do not allow for other, simultaneous, and equally valid principles for classifying the same life forms. By contrast, in contemporary queer taxonomical systems, the core axes of gender, sexual orientation, and relational orientation function as *nonhierarchical and simultaneous lenses* through which different aspects of the same individual might come into view. This is how you get identifications in the form of serial lists, such as "biromantic gay trans man." Each taxon references a discrete axis of personhood and thus may be combined with any term corresponding to another axis. The method of taxonomy is thereby repurposed in the service of combinatorial queerness—an effort to discern, enable, and incite the range of variations hitherto housed within the two "coarse axes" of gender and sexuality alone (Sedgwick 1990: 22). It is tempting, then, to regard these new taxonomies as significant departures from scientific taxonomies and as examples of what Sedgwick lauds as "nonce taxonomies," which Jack Halberstam (1998: 47) glosses as "ever more accurate or colorful or elaborate or imaginative or flamboyant taxonomies."

Hirschfeld's Combinatorial Sublime

We might hold our applause, however, to note that this combinatorial use of taxonomy is neither new nor divorced from taxonomy's scientific and specifically sexological uses. Combinatorial queerness finds a precedent in Hirschfeld's ([1910] 1991) chapter "The Theory of Intermediaries." Famously, Hirschfeld sought to use his authority as a German sexologist (which was continually under fire, since he was both Jewish and homosexual) to defend sexual minorities as natural variations rather than either criminals or pathologies. In "The Theory of Intermediaries," Hirschfeld hypothesizes that just as there is natural variation on an anatomical level between male bodies, female bodies, and intersex bodies, there is also naturally occurring biological variation with regard to every other aspect of sex. Hirschfeld's project is to taxonomize every facet of sex as a means of mapping the range of possible variations from a strict sex binary. His system begins with four basic categories, whose rough contemporary translations are as follows: "1. the sexual organs," or genitals and gonads; "2. the other physical characteristics," or secondary sex characteristics; "3. the sex drive," or sexual and romantic orientation, courtship style, and sexual position; and "4. the other emotional characteristics," or gender expression (Hirschfeld [1910] 1991: 219).

Just as with new queer taxonomies, Hirschfeld's four basic axes are *mobile*—any element of each axis may be combined with any element of any of the three others. To illustrate this with mathematical precision, Hirschfeld includes three tables intended to detail the range of combinations of these four types, each of which might occur in three variations labeled with the subscripts m, w, or m+w, which correspond to *man, woman,* or *mixture of both,* which is to say sexual intermediary. Fully tabulated, there are eighty-one possible sexual variations. But that is not all. Hirschfeld notes that each of the basic four axes could be further subdivided into four finer distinctions. For instance, he divides the sex drive into (1) orientation (to women, men, womanly men, manly women, older, younger, etc.), (2) approach ("whether aggressively courting or alluring"), (3) disposition ("rooted partly in the emotional, partly in the sensual"—a gendered precursor to asexual distinctions between romantic, sensual, and sexual modes of attraction), and (4) manner of activity ("active or passive") (226). With these additional subdivisions factored in, the total number of possible combinations ascends to 43,046,721, which Hirschfeld estimates to be approximately one-third of the total world population at the time. Hirschfeld claims that this number is still "too small," proposing that if we were to divide each of the four subdivisions into two finer subdivisions (for instance, under "4. the other emotional characteristics," dividing gendered clothing into outer garments versus undergarments), "then the amount of possibilities of sexual varieties would overtake the number of the world population" (227).

In the intoxication with numbers begetting numbers through proliferating subdivisions, Hirschfeld instrumentalizes taxonomy to achieve a version of combinatorial queerness limned by the mathematical sublime. The intent behind this endless multiplication is a recognition of the astounding range of human sexual diversity, a diversity that stretches toward the infinite because, in Hirschfeld's view, individual humans are biologically singular: "The number of actual and imaginable sexual varieties is almost unending; in each person there is a different mixture of manly and womanly substances, and as we cannot find two leaves alike on a tree, then it is highly unlikely that we will find two humans whose manly and womanly characteristics exactly match in kind and number" (228). Here, combinatorial queerness stretches toward the utopian horizon of universal transness. For, upon reading Hirschfeld, it becomes clear that sexual intermediaries—womanly men and manly women—do not only include homosexuals, bisexuals, transvestites, and (in the language of the time) hermaphrodites; they also include such characters as the woman writer who prefers sensitive or even homosexual men, the sensitive male artist, the older woman who prefers younger men, the man who prefers big-boned Germanic women, and so on (Hirschfeld 2000). In short, "normal" heterosexuality is gradually emptied of its content as ever more of its avatars are reclassified as sexual intermediaries. Hirschfeld reveals the entirely manly man and the entirely womanly woman to be extremely rare biological specimens, if not fictive ideals altogether.

One could be forgiven for wondering whether Hirschfeld's turn to taxonomy's regularizing and classificatory conventions to prove that humans are individually unique is not ultimately contradictory and even wrongheaded. To explain this, it is worth emphasizing that in the early twentieth-century biological sciences, *taxonomy is science itself*. To taxonomize is to claim a certain scientificity without which one's work would lack truthiness and universality. Hirschfeld thus turns to the combined methods of taxonomy, mathematics, and tabulation in a bid to convey the notion that "people are different from one another" in terms consonant with the truth games of science.

Taxonomy's Epistemological Inheritances

What are we to make of the untimely echoes between Hirschfeld's and contemporary queer uses of the taxonomical method? The utopian horizon of both taxonomic systems is nearly coextensive with the uniqueness of each individual. Undergraduates regularly tell me, unknowingly echoing Hirschfeld, that *there are as many genders and sexualities as there are people*. One conclusion might see an unacknowledged tradition of deploying taxonomical thinking in the service of queer, trans, and asexual world-making projects. This tradition could include Michael Dillon (2013)—a white stealth trans man who became an early twentieth-century American endocrinologist and devised a classificatory schema sorting "masculine female inverts," for whom medical transition was indicated, from "mannish female inverts," for whom it was not—and Virginia Prince, a midcentury white American transvestite who authored her own sexological studies and devised her own taxonomical system. Another, less sanguine conclusion could be that Hirschfeld exposes the sexological roots of contemporary queer taxonomies and, in so doing, prompts us to interrogate the utopian aspirations that animate them. To take the latter conclusion seriously is not necessarily to claim that taxonomy has been irreparably tainted by the history of unsavory uses to which it has been put. After all, methods, terminologies, and even institutional fields need not be bound by their pasts and might, under certain conditions, be turned to new aims. What proves harder to shake than the historical uses of taxonomy, however, are its epistemological premises.

Taxonomy's biological inheritance brings with it the conceit that taxonomical categories and divisions are objective and innate, the hidden laws that govern what manifests in the natural world. This is the foundational premise of Hirschfeld's taxonomy: that everything—from choice of hobbies, to aptitude for a certain profession, to gait, to taste in undergarments, to preference for certain sex acts, to attraction to cavalrymen—is ultimately biologically determined, albeit according to sexed elements that are far more complex and variable than mere binary genital anatomy. Despite the ethos of self-identification and rejection of outside (or insider) experts classifying individuals according to "objective" criteria, new queer taxonomies end up dovetailing, sometimes intentionally (Chasin 2013), with popular and medical beliefs that sexual and gender identities are biologically rooted, innate, unchanging, and discrete from one another. This, in turn, reinforces damaging, exclusionary, and grossly oversimplified criteria about who counts as, for instance, a "true" transsexual or authentic asexual. Indeed, the vernacular thirst to taxonomize partakes of a scientism that animates faith in taxonomy as a significant and meaningful method in the first place. Just as Hirschfeld deployed taxonomy to put the universalist power of science behind the notion that sexed individuality is infinitely diverse, new queer classification systems use taxonomy to make an implicit bid for the rationality, legibility, and scientific validity of otherwise quirky outsider identities.

Hirschfeld's taxonomy is based in the theory that universal bisexuality (shared anatomical structures that may later differentiate into male and female) is the lowest form of development, both on the scale of individual organisms and within evolution itself. This theory underpinned understandings of racialized people as less sexually differentiated and thus less evolved than the white races, just as it underwrote conceptions of white sexual deviants as regressions heralding white devolution. Moreover, Hirschfeld's descriptive definitions of "manly" and "womanly" traits—the basis of his entire system—elevate white northern European ideals of both gendered behavior and racial phenotype to the status of universal biological principles. These aspects, however, could be corrected in revised sexual taxonomies, and in fact, new queer taxonomies leave them behind. Instead, it is *taxonomy's implicit bid for universal validity* that serves as the carrier of the method's racist and colonialist histories. New spins on taxonomy risk installing a new universalism that downgrades competing epistemologies to the status of the local, the backward, the traditional, or the false conflation. David Valentine's (2007) caution that the category *transgender*, and the North American presuppositions that come with it, might become a new Western progress narrative masquerading as a universalist ontology should be extended to these new classification systems. The fact that new queer taxonomies initially emerged from middle-class, majority white communities in the global North means that the possibility that they could achieve something like a universal ontological status must be taken seriously. Epistemologies that lack access to universalist truth-value due to racial and geographical hierarchies of knowledge and that fail or refuse to speak within the secular and scientific idioms of rationality could be elbowed out in the process. New queer taxonomies may not be the nonce taxonomies Sedgwick had in mind. After all, what makes a taxonomy "nonce" for Sedgwick is not just its vernacular provenance. It is, more importantly, the fact that it is "unsystematic," descriptive, "provisional," ephemeral, local, and plural rather than comprehensive, systematic, and universal (Sedgwick 1990: 23). All cultures divide the complexity of the social into more manageable groupings of like and unlike. Only universalist taxonomies pretend that their divisions are *the best*—that is, not only the most rational and the truest, but also the most descriptively fitted to natural human variety such that, unlike other modes of categorization, they accurately match, rather than uncomfortably curtailing, the makeup of each individual.

The universalist ambitions of new queer taxonomies break sharply with prior queer vernaculars in the United States. For one example, we can turn to what historian Joanne Meyerowitz (2002: 169) has called the "taxonomical revolution" of the 1960s, in which sexual subcultures "sorted" themselves out in light of the new self-making possibilities unlocked by hormones and "sex change" surgeries. Aside from *transsexual* and *transvestite*, the terms that emerged from this vernacular ferment—such as *drag queens*, *street queens*, and *hormone queens*—were emphatically nonscientific and nongeneralizable, and they drew on everyday speech in the gay world (192–94). It is immediately evident that this 1960s vernacular was based more on *what you did* than who you were: a hormone queen took estrogen; a transsexual got a sex change. Arguably, in the gay world (contra medical epistemologies), the fact that a transsexual was considered a woman and a hormone queen was not was the consequence of the former's sex change operation rather than of her internal identity. Significantly, *what you did* included not just hormones, surgery, and clothing, but also occupation: a drag queen was a performer, and a street queen was often assumed to be a prostitute. In short, the 1960s gay/transfeminine vernacular describes external behaviors that generate identity effects and draws on terms—such as *queen*—that bear the indelible mark of time-and-place-bound subcultures. By way of contrast, the new queer taxonomy's investment in rational quasiscientific taxonomies of *being* (not behavior) is startling.

Even closer to the present are those queer vernaculars most recently superseded or incorporated by the new system. Some of the terms that I was aware of in Durham, North Carolina, in the early aughts included *faggot, queer, dyke, butch, femme, stud, aggressive, genderqueer, boi, tranny, transfaggot,* and *trannyfaggot.* Of these, *genderqueer* is the only one that is consistently included as a gender identity within contemporary classification systems, no doubt in honor of its status as a precursor to *nonbinary.* Overall, however, these vernacular terms were precisely that; they hardly amounted to anything so grandiose as a classification system, much less a taxonomy. Prominent among them were identities such as *stud, aggressive, faggot, butch,* and *femme* that implied gender expression and sexuality simultaneously. A faggot was effeminate, flamboyant, and sexually oriented to men and masculinity; a butch was masculine, stoic, and sexually oriented to women and femininity. Also prominent (and consistent with the history of queer vernaculars) were reclaimed insults, including all manner of variations on *queer, faggot, dyke,* and *tranny.* By contrast, the new classification system's bid for taxonomical rationality is evident in its purging of terms that imply gender and sexuality simultaneously (for the separation of these axes is the basis of the entire system) as well as reclaimed insults (for there is nothing universal about a faggot). What replaces them is a quasiscientific and affectively neutral series of terms that aims for the greatest possible precision regarding location on the gender spectrum. The nonbinary "umbrella" thereby includes terms such as *gender fluid, agender, bigender, neutrois,* and *pangender.* To be clear, young people *do* continue to use some of the older terms. What interests me is the fact that, despite their continuing use, older vernaculars (again, aside from *genderqueer*) most often do not make their way into contemporary internet listicles of gender identities. This is significant because graphs and listicles are precisely the locations where vernaculars are converted into taxonomies. When older terms, such as *butch* and *femme,* do make it onto these listicles, it is as mere gender expressions, *not* authentic genders or sexualities—a radical curtailment of their field of meaning.

Tellingly, racial, geographical, and historical alterity are either ignored or incorporated into new queer taxonomies rather than being treated as potential vectors of epistemological difference or, in Macharia's words cited earlier, as simply "not related" to classifications that originate in sexology. As many users remarked upon its rollout, Facebook's extensive menu of gender options does not include *butch* or *femme*. The presumption seems to be that *butch* and *femme* have been historically superseded by *transgender*, *nonbinary*, and *cisgender*, and that butches and femmes ought to simply recategorize themselves. Unsurprisingly, Facebook's menu does not include Black genders such as *stud*, *aggressive*, or *femme queen*, much less genders understood to be "cultural" and "traditional" such as *hijra*, *bakla*, or *travesti*, to name just a few. Other listicles aspiring to be comprehensive might include some of these terms (and, interestingly, almost all include *two-spirit*), but my point is that this is a problem not best solved by inclusivity. Genuine epistemological difference is enabled by contexts that are about more than gender, such as kinship, cosmology, political sovereignty, race, class, labor, and yes, sexuality. To incorporate such difference as a specimen under the rubric of types of gender identity can amount to an additional settler/colonial violence.[3] This deracinated, decontextualized, universalist settler whiteness is the most dangerous inheritance contemporary queer taxonomies take from the problematic history of scientific taxonomy.

But even this need not be a definitive condemnation. I want to acknowledge the creative and resourceful ways in which Indigenous and racialized people "disidentify" with these categories, creatively reworking them and exposing their normative operations from within (Muñoz 1999). Such disidentificatory performances occur every time an Indigenous or racialized person lays claim to one of these categories while calling attention to the fact that theirs are usually not the bodies evoked by this category, and even that, racially speaking, they may not have access to cisgender binaries or ideals about "healthy" levels of sexual desire in the first place. I am particularly interested in the ways in which newer categories may be translated into onto-epistemological frameworks that explode their sexological premises, such as historically and culturally resonant understandings of gender as contextual, rather than an internal property of the self, and ontologies of gender as a relation to the divine or the spirit world. I am imaginatively hailed by Afghan-Australian Bobuq Sayed's reference to their nonbinary identity as "contextual" (Aranjuez 2017). What does it mean to translate a contemporary term from the global North, such as *nonbinary*, into the culturally and historically resonant practice of shifting between modes of gendered selfhood in relation to the contexts— of labor, family, religion, friends, and sexuality—in which one circulates? In such practices, gender is neither, as sexological taxonomy presumes, an innate property of the self nor a distinct axis of identity; rather, it is constituted relationally in and through shifting social worlds. It may, therefore, not constitute either an injury or a deception when, for example, an otherwise transfeminine person consents to being buried, entering a holy space, or attending family functions as a man, as is common in many locations in the global South (Reddy 2005; Boellstorff 2007; Najmabadi 2014).

We might also consider the complex identification of the late drag artist Mildred/Dred Gerestant. In a radically disjunctive and asymmetrical nonce taxonomy that rivals Sedgwick's own, they identified as a "multispirited, Haitian-American, gender-illusioning, Black, shaved, different, God/dess, anti-oppression, open, non-traditional, self-expressed, blessed, gender-bending, drag-kinging, fluid, ancestor-supported and after that, non-labeling Wo/Man" (MacDonald 2010). As Omis'eke Tinsley (2018) explains, Mildred/Dred's theorization of the Haitian roots of their drag practice subjects the term *fluid*—a gender identity included in contemporary queer taxonomies—to the torque of the Vodoun ontology of spirit possession as a means of gendered becoming. Indeed, Mildred/Dred's pronoun of choice, "their," is not a nonbinary singular possessive, but rather a plural possessive, reflecting their understanding of themselves as *a plural being*, inhabited alternately by masculine and feminine spirits. In these examples (and many others), diasporic queers creatively translate taxonomized identities in ways that foil the epistemological premises of sexological taxonomy itself.

Conclusion: Critique and the Ethics of Scholarship

What, then, are we to make of new queer taxonomies? The radical and foundationalist forms of critique in which we are trained in the "identity knowledges" (Wiegman 2012: 1) dispose us to reject outright compromised methods such as taxonomy as culturally imperialist, unqueer, and sexological at heart. Whether or not scholars critique it, however, the queer taxonomical imaginary is likely here to stay. I, for one, find the growing bifurcation of queer, trans, and asexual scholarly analytics from queer, trans, and asexual practices of living frankly unethical. My proposal, then, is threefold. First, "deidealize" queerness by recognizing that taxonomy *can* be queer, in the sense of being useful and meaningful to queer-identified people (Amin 2017). This approach requires cultivating scholarly sympathy and empirical curiosity about the identifications, erotics, relations, and lifeways opened up by new, queer, trans, and asexual taxonomies. Second, continually center those Indigenous, non-Western, and historical ontologies of being that new taxonomies—with their universalist scientific trappings—threaten to erase, incorporate, and/or supersede. Finally, fuck with the universalizing presumptions of the taxonomical method from within by generating idiosyncratic interpretations and translations that explode the epistemological and ontological foundations of taxonomy itself. That, I think, would be an ethical scholarly approach to new queer, trans, and asexual taxonomies.

Notes

1. For an example of a complex graph of the possible relations between romantic orientation and sexual orientation, see Diehm 2017.

2. Przybylo (2019) notes, without resolving, this tension between asexuality as a legitimate sexual orientation and asexuality as a challenge to compulsory sexuality. Snaza (2020) argues that asexuality as an identity shuts down the more generative possibilities of asexuality as a queer relation to sexual and relational norms.

3. See Driskill 2016 on the inseparability of Indigenous gender/sexual identities from land, medicine, and spirituality.

References

Amin, Kadji. 2017. *Disturbing Attachments: Genet, Modern Pederasty, and Queer History.* Durham, NC: Duke University Press.

Aranjuez, Adolfo. 2017. "Interview #9—Bobuq Sayed." *LIMINAL*, May 15. https://www .liminalmag.com/interviews/bobuq-sayed.

Boellstorff, Tom. 2007. *A Coincidence of Desires: Anthropology, Queer Studies, Indonesia.* Durham, NC: Duke University Press.

Butler, Judith. 1999. *Gender Trouble: Feminism and the Subversion of Identity.* New York: Routledge.

Chasin, CJ DeLuzio. 2013. "Reconsidering Asexuality and Its Radical Potential." *Feminist Studies* 39, no. 2: 405–26. http://www.jstor.org/stable/23719054.

"Collective Identity Model." n.d. AVENwiki. http://wiki.asexuality.org/Collective_identity _model.

Diehm, Jan. 2017. "The Asexual Spectrum: Identities in the Ace Community (INFO-GRAPHIC)." *HuffPost*, December 6. https://www.huffpost.com/entry/asexual -spectrum_n_3428710.

Dillon, Michael. 2013. *Self: A Study in Ethics and Endocrinology.* London: Butterworth-Heinemann.

Driskill, Qwo-Li. 2016. *Asegi Stories: Cherokee Queer and Two-Spirit Memory.* Tucson: University of Arizona Press.

Foucault, Michel. (1976) 1990. *The History of Sexuality: An Introduction.* New York: Vintage Books.

Ghaziani, Amin, and Matt Brim, eds. 2019. *Imagining Queer Methods*. New York: New York University Press.

Gill-Peterson, Jules. 2018. *Histories of the Transgender Child*. Minneapolis: University of Minnesota Press.

Halberstam, Jack. 1998. *Female Masculinity*. Durham, NC: Duke University Press.

Hayward, Eva, and Jami Weinstein. 2015. "Introduction: Tranimalities in the Age of Trans* Life." *TSQ: Transgender Studies Quarterly* 2, no. 2: 195–208.

Hirschfeld, Magnus. (1910) 1991. *Transvestites: The Erotic Drive to Cross-Dress*, translated by Michael Lombardi-Nash. Amherst, NY: Prometheus Books.

Hirschfeld, Magnus. 2000. *The Homosexuality of Men and Women*, translated by Michael Lombardi-Nash. Amherst, NY: Prometheus Books.

Jackson, Zakiyyah Iman. 2020. *Becoming Human: Matter and Meaning in an Antiblack World*. New York: New York University Press.

Lafleur, Greta. 2018. *The Natural History of Sexuality in Early America*. Baltimore, MD: Johns Hopkins University Press.

Love, Heather. 2015. "Doing Being Deviant: Deviance Studies, Description, and the Queer Ordinary." *Differences: A Journal of Feminist Cultural Studies* 26, no. 1: 74–95.

MacDonald, Kristy. 2010. *Assume Nothing: MilDred Gerestant*. November 1. https://www.youtube.com/watch?v=pWAg3DsEnaA.

Macharia, Keguro. 2020. "Belated: Interruption." *GLQ* 26, no. 3: 561–73.

Meyerowitz, Joanne. 2002. *How Sex Changed: A History of Transsexuality in the United States*. Cambridge, MA: Harvard University Press.

Mitra, Durba. 2020. *Indian Sex Life: Sexuality and the Colonial Origins of Modern Social Thought*. Princeton, NJ: Princeton University Press.

Muñoz, José Esteban. 1999. *Disidentifications: Queers of Color and the Performance of Politics*. Minneapolis: University of Minnesota Press.

Najmabadi, Afsaneh. 2014. *Professing Selves: Transsexuality and Same-Sex Desire in Contemporary Iran*. Durham, NC: Duke University Press.

Przybylo, Ela. 2019. *Asexual Erotics: Intimate Readings of Compulsory Sexuality*. Columbus: Ohio State University Press.

Reddy, Gayatri. 2005. *With Respect to Sex: Negotiating Hijra Identity in South India*. Chicago: University of Chicago Press.

Ross, Marlon. 2005. "Beyond the Closet as Raceless Paradigm." In *Black Queer Studies: A Critical Anthology*, edited by E. Patrick Johnson and Mae G. Henderson, 161–89. Durham, NC: Duke University Press.

Sedgwick, Eve Kosofsky. 1990. *Epistemology of the Closet*. Berkeley: University of California Press.

Snaza, Nathan. 2020. "Asexuality and Erotic Biopolitics." *Feminist Formations* 32, no. 3: 121–44.

Stein, Melissa. 2015. *Measuring Manhood: Race and the Science of Masculinity, 1830–1934.* Minneapolis: University of Minnesota Press.

Stryker, Susan, Paisley Currah, and Lisa Jean Moore. 2008. "Introduction: Trans-, Trans, or Transgender?" *WSQ: Women's Studies Quarterly* 36, no. 3–4: 11–22.

Tinsley, Omise'eke. 2018. *Ezili's Mirrors: Imagining Black Queer Genders.* Durham, NC: Duke University Press.

Valentine, David. 2007. *Imagining Transgender: An Ethnography of a Category.* Durham, NC: Duke University Press.

Wiegman, Robyn. 2012. *Object Lessons.* Durham, NC: Duke University Press.

GAY GENES IN THE POSTGENOMIC ERA

A Roundtable

**Stephanie D. Clare, Patrick R. Grzanka,
and Joanna Wuest**

$\mathcal{I}$n a paper published in *Science* in September 2019 to global fanfare, geneticist Andrea Ganna and his multidisciplinary team's genome-wide association study (GWAS) identified five loci of genetic material associated with same-sex sexual activity among a large American and British sample of people of European ancestry (Ganna et al. 2019). First performed in 2002, the GWAS method identifies, across the entire human genome, genetic variations—mostly single-nucleotide polymorphisms (SNPs, pronounced "snips")—that correlate with particular traits, such as behaviors or personality types (Ikegawa 2012: 221). This approach was made possible by the mapping of the human genome and the consequent widespread availability of complete human genome sequences; thus, the GWAS is designated as a postgenomic method. Unlike late-twentieth-century hereditary and monocausal explanations of "homosexuality" advanced by scientists including Simon LeVay, Dean Hamer, and J. Michael Bailey, a GWAS is able to estimate the influence of potential genetic markers across the entire human genome using staggeringly large sample sizes and statistical methods. That said, identification of common SNPs associated with a particular trait does not mean that people with these SNPs will necessarily exhibit that trait. In this case, drawing on over 450,000 individuals' genetic material from the UK Biobank and 23andMe, Ganna and colleagues' findings purportedly constituted groundbreaking evidence of the complex gene-environment interactions that produce phenotypes, though the aggregate percentage of variation in same-sex sexual behavior explained by the five genetic loci was very small (8–25 percent) and an unreliable predictor of sexual behav-

GLQ 29:1
DOI 10.1215/10642684-10144449
© 2023 by Duke University Press

ior. Even then, the study framed itself as revealing the "genetic architecture"—which is to say the blueprint or design—of same-sex sexual behavior.

The study's conclusions were unsurprising and unremarkable: ultimately the authors concluded that "many loci with individually small effects," spread across the entire genome, contribute in statistically significant but highly unpredictable ways to an individual's sexual behavior. In other words, genes contribute minimally, inconsistently, and complexly to human sexual expression. What is remarkable, however, is the authors' and journal editors' sense of the study's importance and the ways the study's self-identification as important was interpolated in the pages of *Science* and in broader public discourse. Regardless of whether geneticists *or* queer studies scholars interpreted the findings to be mundane, the study's impact was practically predetermined to be deeply consequential and global in scope.

Ganna and colleagues consulted with activists and communications experts during the implementation and rollout of the study in an attempt to preempt both the co-optation of their work for political means and the misinterpretation of their findings. The research team organized workshops with groups such as the Peter Tatchell Foundation and London Pride, which helped to anticipate and minimize political fallout. Representatives from GLAAD and other national LGBTQ+ organizations read drafts, provided feedback, and helped frame the language of the findings and their public release. The team even worked with a professional consultant, UK-based science communicators Sense about Science, and subsequently pushed the editors at *Science* to use images, videos, and an FAQ on the genetics of sexual orientation to accompany the published article. The energy spent on communicating the findings betrays that at least some members of the team were concerned with the potential (mis)use of their findings in public discourse and social policy.

In this roundtable, we each offer a perspective on the GWAS informed by queer studies and our distinct disciplinary orientations and methods. Together, we argue that the 2019 GWAS marks a moment of both flux and continuity: a recognition of sexuality's complexity and contingency alongside a continued belief in biology's role in telling fundamental truths about behavior and identity. The roundtable begins with Patrick R. Grzanka, who suggests attention to affect reveals how the postgenomic science of sexuality is as mired in deep investments in biology and etiological narratives of where sexual desires come from as are the earlier, monocausal explanations it supposedly jettisons. We then turn to Joanna Wuest's political economic perspective, which uncovers both the truth *and* the absurdity in the notion that postgenomics has taken us beyond the "born this way" ideology. We end with Stephanie Clare, who argues that the GWAS's treatment of "sex," defined as a binary system of male and female, is insufficient for understanding nonheterosexual sexual behavior and could be used to buttress arguments that use the legitimacy of science to fight trans rights. This treatment of "sex" indexes how, even as the GWAS breaks from a biocentric model of the human, at the same time it retains aspects of this model and maintains what Sylvia Wynter calls the "overrepresentation of Man." From our different vantages, our work converges around the notion that processes of reification—that is, those broader social forces that work before, after, and upon how the study is conceived, conducted, and published—best explain the persistent search for genetic determinants of sexual behavior.

Patrick R. Grzanka: "Programs of Life/Knowing Ourselves"

I knew Ganna et al.'s study would be important, because it claimed to be so different from much of the sexual orientation science of the recent past, particularly the high-profile and highly controversial work of Hamer, Bailey, LeVay, and others, as well as prior studies with insufficient samples to detect significant effects. Since then, as part of my new book project, I have been conducting what Sara Ahmed (2006: 105) called an "ethnography of texts." Through interviews with study personnel and analysis of the paper's uptake in public discourse, I have been tracing the social lives of the GWAS. By following it around, I have shifted my own attention away from what *the data say* about the genetic foundations of sexual behavior and toward what is said *about and around the data*. Of course, data do not speak for themselves, but instead are spoken about and spoken for in the name of particular aims. I am especially concerned with discourse about Ganna et al.'s GWAS, including what the social actors who were involved in and encountered the GWAS say about it.

As we noted, the authors choreographed the study's release with input from nonscientist activists and science communications experts. Though the text of the study itself is vague, the authors reference the "long history of misusing genetic results for social purposes" (Ganna et al. 2019: 7). Sociologist and study coauthor Robbee Wedow wrote with biologist and study coauthor Stephen Phelps in the *New York Times* that "yes, your sex life is influenced by your genes. . . . The study's findings also complicate the relationship between genetics and sexuality" (Phelps and Wedow 2019). How precisely the findings would "complicate" this relationship became the focus of intense public relations work, practices that are relatively unusual for papers ostensibly about correlations between SNPs and traits. The work was always political, of course, because the authors sought to clarify a scientific question about a socially contentious topic (i.e., what *is* the genetic contribution to same-sex behavior?), and the findings practically invite misinterpretation. Wedow and colleagues knew they were releasing their conclusions about the genetic architecture of same-sex behavior amid intense debates about the nature and origins of sexual orientation that play out in courts, laboratories, and broader popular discourse—what I called the "'born this way' wars" (Grzanka 2018).

Predictably, the headlines soon followed: "There's no one 'gay gene,'" (*Washington Post*), "Scientists quash idea of single 'gay gene'" (*Guardian*), and "'Gay gene' ruled out" (*Telegraph*). Though the news coverage was typically more clarifying than the clickbait headlines suggest, the gestalt of reporting on Ganna's findings announced the end of the hunt for the gay gene, as if a mythical odyssey had been abruptly interrupted by an inconvenient truth. Indeed, the thrust of the GWAS was that several parts of the genome contributed to some small amount of variance in same-sex behavior that appears to be context-specific, further invalidating the notion that a singular gene contained the secret of sexual orientation's origins. Given the ubiquity of biological explanations of behavior (Panofsky 2014), the headlines could be read as contrarian or ironic. But another way of thinking about them is that they simultaneously evoke and confront an *affective investment* in bioessentialism: a public feeling, a structural, political, and deeply felt attachment to biomedical renderings of the self that have a contingent relationship to actual scientific knowledge.

For example, according to the scientific record, the gay gene had never actually been discovered, but the gay gene hypothesis nonetheless took on a mythic status during the 1990s and 2000s (Wuest 2021; see Hegarty 1997 for the related gay brain). The ascendance of the gay gene corresponded with a range of sociohistorical and cultural factors that may have influenced a shift in attitudes toward gay and lesbian people. In the context of the HIV/AIDS pandemic, increased representation of white cisgender gay and lesbian people in popular culture (Schiappa, Gregg, and Hewes 2006), the rise of attribution theory in psychology (Kelley 1967), and LGBTQ+ activists' efforts to stop so-called conversion therapy (Waidzunas and Epstein 2015), biogenetic explanations for homosexual behavior became hegemonic. As many others have elaborated (Epstein 1987; Walters 2014), the gay gene became a kind of biologizing trick, yoking a scientifically imagined biodeterminism to sexual minority rights. By the time Lady Gaga's single of that name was released in 2011, "born this way" was as much a reflection of pervasive cultural beliefs as it was a political intervention, calcifying a doxa that was as much affective as empirical.

Even as public understanding of postgenomic science may be underin-

Figure 1. Image from First Stone Ministries, "New Study Reveals—AGAIN—No One Is Born Gay!" February 25, 2022. https://www.firststone.org /articles/post/new-study-reveals -no-one-born-gay.

formed or misguided, the GWAS both complicates and reiterates expert and lay sexual knowledges. On the one hand, the newsworthiness attributed to Ganna's GWAS lies in its rejection of a singular genetic determinist account of sexuality in exchange for a scientifically sophisticated and empirically substantiated post-genomic paradigm. From this vantage, it may be tempting to position the GWAS as orthogonal to the gay brain, twin studies, and what Waidzunas and Epstein (2015) called earlier "truth devices" (e.g., phallometric testing), whereby the latter are determinist and reductionist and the GWAS is nuanced and multidimensional. From a strictly scientific perspective, this may indeed be an accurate characterization of how the evidence produced by the GWAS refutes earlier, invalid accounts of sexual orientation's etiology.

Headlines in the popular press announcing the results of Ganna et al.'s GWAS index a public understanding of homosexuality that would be unsettled, if not threatened, by the disappearance of the gay gene. Whether or not the gay gene hypothesis had any actual effect on anti-LGBTQ+ religious conservative groups' beliefs or behavior, its rejection was celebrated by at least some proponents of conversion therapy. For example, an evangelical Christian website produced this image (see fig. 1) alongside a column about Ganna's GWAS. Reading the paper as proof that no one is born gay, sexual orientation change advocate Stephen Black said that "gay advocates will also try to spin this to communicate that 'conversion therapy'—talk therapy to help people overcome homosexuality—is bad" (Otis 2019). Black, who identifies as having come "out of homosexuality 37 years ago," said Ganna's findings merely verify what "most Christians have been saying all along": "When anyone engages in sexual immorality, it physically changes brain structure, not the other way around" (Otis 2019). Ganna and colleagues' concerns about their work being weaponized—as justification for "discrimination on the basis of sexual identity and attraction" (Ganna et al. 2019: 6)—is at least partially substantiated by Black's work *and* by headlines in the popular press. With no gay gene to be found and a burgeoning epigenetic framework that actually does reject the deterministic logic that gay people are born gay, the GWAS could buttress arguments for or *against* LGBTQ+ rights, particularly in terms of sexual orientation's perceived immutability (Diamond and Rosky 2016), despite well-intentioned efforts to mitigate against such a response.

While ex-gay Black's political ambitions and relationship to science are unquestionably divergent from geneticist Ganna's, there is a strange affinity within at least the rhetoric of their conclusions. For example, Ganna told me that, in contrast with lay beliefs in genetic determinism, he and his colleagues hope to use the GWAS to show how "if you change the environment, the genetics change." Specifically, he pointed to his team's findings that same-sex sexual behavior is associated with risk-taking, which he associated with societal heterosexism, that is, one has to risk social ostracism in order to act on same-sex desires. "But what if you live in a society where you don't need to be a risk taker to engage in same-sex behavior?" he proposed. "Then that genetic signal that was determining same-sex behavior is not going to exist anymore. It just disappears, because the environment has changed." Here, epigenetics, as viewed through the lens of the GWAS, help expose the profound mutability of the genome and of sexuality, though hardly the kind of conditioned mutability proposed by coercive sexual orientation change advocates. Ganna conveyed a strong sense of the genome's plasticity and of the immense amount of data required to estimate even small amounts of variance in outcomes. He told me that when it comes to sexual orientation, "some is environment, some is genetic, and I think it's nothing unexpected with that and fits my expectations and my observations." Wedow said similarly, "There shouldn't be anything shocking or unpredicted even [about the GWAS], given what we know about behavioral outcomes." These dispassionate accounts of "highly predictable" sexual epigenetics are in stark contrast with the bombast of evangelical conversion therapy proponents *and* LGBTQ+ activists, a point of which both Ganna and Wedow seemed acutely aware. Yet, these distinct constituencies, Christian conversion therapy proponents and postgenomic scientists, wind up in an epistemic affinity—"no one born gay," as a headline on Black's website put it (Otis 2019)—that might disquiet especially the scientists who view GWAS techniques as possessing a politically liberatory potential. Furthermore, if their findings were so obvious, then why was the study so important?

The explosion of attention directed at this paper sparked the mandatory questions for considering the politics of biomedical knowledge: what knowledge? Whose knowledge? For what ends? To borrow from Steven Epstein (2020), I also think reactions to Ganna's GWAS demand an interrogation of the affective dimensions of our "epistemic attachments." Geneticist Shiro Ikegawa (2012: 240) wrote that the technology undergirding the GWAS has produced "the most spectacular results of the human genome study." Ikegawa asserted that the GWAS exposes our "program of life": "This knowledge (knowing ourselves) is revolutionizing medicine" (240). What kind of program of life had Ganna, Wedow, and colleagues actually uncovered? And how would these programs be taken up as knowledge (*knowing ourselves*)?

It is imperative to consider how lay and authoritative discourse about the mysteries of the genome and its associations with sexual behaviors rearticulate affective investments in sexuality's elusive biogenetic foundations (Grzanka 2019). The GWAS was received as groundbreaking, but its own authors described the findings as unsurprising and totally predictable. It was as if the mystery of sexual orientation was not a mystery at all; it was just hidden out of sight, waiting to be discovered. In that case, are the sexual epigenetics described by Ganna et al. (2019) actually a rejection of biogenetic essentialism as an epistemic framework—a new program of knowledge—or a reconstitution? Beyond the recalcitrant essentialist/constructionist or nature/nurture binaries, these new approaches to genomic mapping recalibrate long-standing "born this way" logics in terms of technoscientifically laden attachments to the science of sexual desires: inputs and outputs, on and off switches. The authors of the GWAS study do not claim to have discovered sexual orientation in the genome; epistemically, they do not think such a discovery is even possible. In turn, their work effectively circumvents questions about sexual *orientation* while nonetheless claiming (authoritative) knowledge about sexual *desires* and *behavior*. The evidence has shifted and the conclusions have been modified substantially from the work of Hamer, LeVay, and others who envisioned a much more hereditary and identitarian framing of sexuality (e.g., *gay* brothers beget *gay* brothers). And yet the GWAS still purports to identify the biological matter that influences what makes a body queer—or at least what makes some bodies have nonheterosexual sex. There's not one gay gene, and the GWAS negates even the possibility of such a proposition. Nevertheless, the practitioners of these genome-wide analyses herald the technology's capacity to reveal our program of life—to show us the knowledge of ourselves. Given the hegemonic status of "born this way" ideology and the alleged power of the GWAS to expose what has been obscured by earlier sciences, might the new sexual postgenomics fail to constitute what Michel Foucault (1970) referred to as an epistemic break in the order of things, and instead represent the evolution of a knowledge project rooted firmly, consistently, in the biomedicalization of everything?

Joanna Wuest: "The Dream of Bioessentialism Is Alive in a Postgenomic Era"

What are we to make of a recent genomic investigation that—rather than concluding with a grand statement on biology and predestiny—stresses the significant role that *sociocultural factors* may play in shaping an individual's penchant for same-sex relations? While public discourse about the 2019 GWAS has generally been framed in light of earlier quests for the fabled "gay gene," the most striking parallels are actually between studies that balanced social and biological factors, which flourished between the mid-1960s and the early 1980s (Kendler 2019). In placing the Ganna et al. GWAS in the context of its antecedents, we might grasp which changes in the political economy of scientific research, civil rights advocacy, and culture writ large have led some to believe that biological origins stories for sexual orientation have lost much of their allure. To the contrary, a deeper inspection of the GWAS and its reception reveals how bioessentialist ideology—that is, the theory that genetics, hormones, or neuroanatomical factors play *the* determinative role in what it means to be a man or a woman, gay or straight, cisgender or trans—has endured. This perspective demonstrates how, despite an uptick in talk of "gender fluidity" and a renewed interest in the "spectrum of sexuality," the domains of science, culture, and politics have not abandoned such essentialist thinking just yet.

Decades before geneticists would plumb the human genome in search of simple gene-to-trait relationships, psychiatrist and onetime president of the American Psychiatric Association Judd Marmor strove to understand homosexuality's complex nature and origins. An early skeptic of the psychoanalytic notion that homosexuality constituted a pathology, Marmor's multiple causes thesis was an attempt to oust the pathological model's peddlers while balancing a range of etiological factors (including once-neglected biological hypotheses). In expounding sexuality's sundry roots, Marmor (1965: 5) introduced his edited volume, *Sexual Inversion: The Multiple Roots of Homosexuality*, with the observation that researchers and clinicians "are probably dealing with a condition that is not only multiply determined by psychodynamic, sociocultural, biological, and situational factors but also reflects the significance of subtle temporal, qualitative, and quantitative variables." In a preface to his collection *Homosexual Behavior*, Marmor (1980: xi) confirmed that "the complex issues surrounding the phenomenon of same-sex object-choice cannot be understood in terms of any unitary cause whether it be biological, psychological, or sociological."

Despite this belief in multiple causes, Marmor steadily granted biological factors preeminence, thereby allowing socio-environmental determinants to recede into the background. Even in his 1965 writings, Marmor (1965: 122–23) enter-tained the notion that a "chromosomal abnormality" might be a *primary* determi-nant of homosexuality. Throughout the 1980s, Marmor posited that intrauterine or early postnatal influence or the hypothalamic centers of the male brain might play some determinative role (Marmor 1980, 1985). By the turn of the millennium, Marmor had become convinced that sexuality was largely biologically determined. In an interview conducted the year before his death, Marmor observed that "we now know that, to a great extent, variations in sexual orientation are determined by the degree of androgenization of the fetal midbrain at a critical period of intra-uterine development," that is, neuroendocrinological causes were key (Rosario 2003: 28).

Marmor's trajectory presents a microcosmic account of how biological renderings of sexuality came to pervade the discourse, though the shift stems from much broader societal transformations. Among these were novel scientific discoveries, an explosion of federal and private funding for biomedical research, and the burgeoning relationships formed between reformist scientists like Mar-mor and the budding gay and lesbian rights movement. Throughout the mid- to late twentieth century, the federal government encouraged biomedical research through expanded university grants and by slashing regulatory restrictions on public-private partnerships (Sunder Rajan 2006; Cooper 2008). Many of these ventures are specifically *biomedical* in nature and work by amassing vast quan-tities of human data (Elwell 2018). For example, biobanks of human DNA and tissues—which are ostensibly compiled for medical research—have functioned as low-lift data mines for testing hypotheses about human difference.

Buttressed by this availability of funding, research into the biologically determined nature of human behavior thrived (Panofsky 2014). Psychologists look-ing to distance themselves from discredited "social contagion" theories embraced biological hypotheses (Bayer 1981), while novel ventures like behavioral genetics and sociobiology capitalized on an influx of grant money. Notably, geneticist and author of the 1993 "gay gene" study Dean Hamer made use of this funding in his pivot from cancer research to a hunt for homosexuality's genetic origins (Hamer and Copeland 1994). On the political front, Marmor and Hamer helped civil rights organizations like the American Civil Liberties Union (ACLU) and the Human Rights Campaign argue that, because gay identities were harmless and immutable, they were worthy of heightened judicial protections and social acceptance alike.

Given the biodeterministic enthusiasm of the past several decades, it was surprising to witness Ganna et al. interpret the 2019 GWAS findings with nuance and humility. Ganna and the other investigators were up front about the limitations of measuring sexuality's incalculable complexities. According to their own hedging, the study's dichotomous variable for sexual behavior "collapses rich and multifaceted diversity among nonheterosexual individuals" (Ganna et al. 2019: 4). Additionally, rather than taking identity as a "thing" in itself, they conceptually distinguished attraction, behavior, and identity as correlated yet distinct. In their own words, the constraints of traditionally operationalized categories surely neglected "the intricacies of the social and cultural influences on sexuality" (3, 10). Could it be that this deep dive into the human genome may have discovered that sociocultural factors might play the greatest role in shaping human sexuality?

However, just as Marmor's balanced considerations belied an incipient bioessentialist turn, the Ganna et al. study was a sign of the biological perspective's tenacity. Although media outlets got the message that the search for a *singular* gay gene had ended years ago along with the most hubristic hypotheses of the Human Genome Project's boosters, they touted the discovery of these new genetic determinants, making scant reference to just how small a role those variants might ultimately play (Belluck 2019). As stalwart defenders of the biological thesis were quick to note, the GWAS did not slam the door on old-school biodeterminism. Indeed, on the study's two-year anniversary, the authors of a similarly designed undertaking trumpeted new insights into the "Darwinian paradox" of same-sex behavior (Zietsch 2021). Even Ganna et al. noted that future research may find additional genetic determinants and related hormonal factors. Ironically, some of the study's most vocal critics even repurposed biodeterministic assumptions for their opprobrium. Whereas Ganna et al. were emphatic that no statistical measure could predict an individual's orientation, researchers affiliated with the Broad Institute condemned the *Science* study for unwittingly inviting future discrimination in the form of gene editing or embryo selection (Gurjao 2019). In the timbre of their rebuke, one can hear an earlier generation of critics' fearful cries about the gay gene's neo-eugenic potential.

There is no shortage of political economic and legal incentives propping up bioessentialist inquiries and ideologies today. It is revealing that 23andMe provided Ganna's team with both personnel and data on the genetic profiles of over one hundred thousand individuals. The DNA home testing firm's economic imperative is to assemble data and market drugs to a consumer base taken by the epistemic promise of bioreductivism. When interviewed about the Ganna et al. GWAS, 23andMe senior scientist Fah Sathirapongsasuti explained that "the study is in part a response to gay, lesbian, and bisexual people's curiosity about themselves. . . . Research and information about sex and sexuality is among the categories most requested by 23andMe's customers" (McIntosh 2019). Just as the race-targeted heart medication BiDil was infamously marketed to African American patients a decade ago, so too has biomedicine been able to make a buck off those eager to learn their genomic personhood (Kahn 2012). In other words, modern research into sexual orientation's genetic nature and origins is in large part a byproduct of the late neoliberal era nexus between investment-driven state policies and the private biomedical industry.

Additionally, LGBTQ+ advocacy organizations continue to find biological narratives useful in thwarting revanchist right-wing litigation groups and conversion therapists who insist that "rapid onset gender dysphoria" and the clinical specter of "irreversible damage" pose an existential threat to young Americans' bodies and fragile psyches (Shrier 2020). In the face of such threats, the National Center for Lesbian Rights continues to promote its "Born Perfect" anti-conversion therapy campaign fit with a not-so-subtle rainbow-hued fingerprint logo, while the ACLU relies on studies of brain structures in transgender individuals in their challenges to anti-transgender policies (Wuest 2019, 2021).

So, what to make of this curious, seemingly incommensurate mixture of persistent bioessentialism on one hand, and Ganna et al.'s rhetorical emphasis on sociocultural factors? Consider that in one of the most robust self-report studies to date, nearly 10 percent of surveyed high schoolers identified as gender diverse, operationalized as any gender identity incongruent with their assigned sex at birth (Kidd et al. 2021). Similarly, a 2021 Gallup poll found that over 15 percent of Generation Z self-categorizes as LGBT (Jones 2021). Might this be evidence that queer identities *are* sensitive to cultural ebbs and flows, and that rising rates of legal protections and visibility have influenced individuals in ways that conservatives have always feared and that liberals—being so wedded to biopolitical legitimation—could hardly afford to consider? When it is less dangerous and more socially acceptable to stray from long-standing gendered and sexual norms, might there be more people who fit under the queer umbrella?

Whether this is an accurate depiction of reality, it has failed to garner influence either in mainstream scientific circles or among LGBTQ+ advocates. In its coverage of the high school gender identity study, the LGBTQ+-themed magazine *them* dismissed the notion that the world was becoming quantitatively queerer. "Experts believe it's not the case that the percentage of people who are transgender is necessarily on the rise," the magazine reported (de la Cretaz 2021). "Rather, as more language has developed for expansive gender identities, and LGBTQ+ visibility and acceptance have increased, more young people feel comfortable openly rejecting the limitations of cisgender identity at an earlier age than they would have otherwise." The core premise here meshes well with bioessentialism, if not an epigenetic variant of its core: more tolerant environments allow for the expression of an underlying queer disposition.

This commonsense sentiment resounds of classical determinism. It divorces a person's "true self" from the self's environment, rendering the two as wholly distinct entities separated by a metaphysical gulf. This is not even an accurate description of how animals and plants express traits in new environments, let alone a plausible account of how intricate human behaviors and identities might spring into being. Thus, the logic of identity with which we are left may be culturally inflected, but it is a closer cousin of its biological ancestor than we might assume. As the reworked narrative goes, we know that queer identity is both multifaceted and anything but inert; however, we also understand identity to be something that is somewhat stable and discernible under a microscope and constituted by an accompanying *telos* that is partially determined by a biological element. Recognitions of complexity and contingency aside, this ought not be mistaken as some wish fulfillment of queer theory. Rather, the postgenomic perspective owes its explanatory power to its inherent flexibility; it is labile enough to accommodate and absorb much critique. Thus, the dream of bioessentialism is still alive in a postgenomic era. What we've inherited is a composite essentialism; a capacious, less rigidly biodeterministic and more socioculturally textured one, but a bioessentialism all the same.

Stephanie Clare: "Biological Sex and the 'Overrepresentation of Man'"

While I read Ganna et al.'s 2019 GWAS as providing a bioinflected queer model of sexuality, one that makes room for some level of complexity and contingency, the study at the very same time treats "sex," as in "male" and "female," as straightforward and self-evident. In this essay, I argue that this treatment of sex clarifies how the GWAS continues in the tradition of the sciences of sexuality as they have been entangled in the coloniality of power (Terry 1999; Somerville 1994; Wynter 2003). Such an understanding of "sex" is both inadequate for understanding sexuality and is an ideological, historical, and culturally contingent effect, one that queer, trans, and scientific communities would do better to contest than to reproduce.

Within the GWAS, the difference between the ways that "sexuality" and "sex" appear is striking. The article describes sexuality as characterized by "multifaced richness and complexity" (Ganna et al. 2019: 6). Eager not to simplify sexuality, the researchers consider "different aspects of sexual orientation and behavior," including the possibility that "attraction, identity, and fantasies" do not neatly align (6). One of their central research questions concerns to what extent genetic influences are the same for same-sex behavior, attraction, fantasy, and identity. In contrast, the authors write that their "analyses and results relate to biologically defined sex, not to gender" (2). The researchers do not explain how they understand "biologically defined sex." This definition is treated as self-evident, but it is foundational to the study: in order to identify same-sex sexual behavior, attraction, identity, and fantasy, they have to have a notion of "same-sexness." Quite simply: the complexity of sexuality in the study rests alongside a framing of "sex" as straightforward and self-evident.

This treatment of sex is problematic for many reasons. First, by not explaining "biologically defined sex," the scientists risk contributing to the understanding of "biological sex" that is often used to cloak intolerance, especially against trans people, with, as Katrina Karkazis (2019: 1899) puts it, the "veneer of science." The study excludes samples from people whose "whose biological sex and self-identified sex/gender" do "not match" (Ganna et al. 2019: 2). The article allows that this is "an important limitation . . . because the analyses do not include transgender persons, intersex persons, and other important persons and groups within the queer community" (2). But it is not the exclusion of trans, intersex, and other people that is the problem (I'm not sure what we might have to gain through inclusion). Rather, the study's representation of sex, especially as highlighted against its treatment of sexuality, gives fodder—likely inadvertently—to the discourses that cite "biological sex" in order to discriminate. For instance, in a leaked memo from 2019, the US Department of Health and Human Services proposed defining sex "on a biological basis that is clear, grounded in science, objective and administrable" and that is "based on immutable biological traits identifiable by or before birth" (Karkazis 2019: 1899). This understanding of biological sex would have nullified Title IX protections for both transgender people and people with differences in sex development. In contrast, Karkazis (2019: 1899) convincingly argues that "we understand sex not as an essential property of individuals but as a set of biological traits and social factors that become important only in specific contexts, such as medicine, and even then complexity persists." Critically, her point is universal: it is not just for some people that sex is not an essential property, but for all of us. This complexity and contextuality are completely covered over in the GWAS.

Building on this point, it is especially striking that the language used in the GWAS makes room for something called "self-identified sex/gender." The inclusion of the word "sex" here is notable. I read it as an implicit nod to the ways in which some transgender activist organizations have argued that constitutional and federal civil rights law ought to "recognize gender identity as a biologically constitutive element of sex" (Wuest 2019: 336). In the context of this GWAS, however, it is significant that the researchers maintain "sex as biologically defined" as separate not only from "self-identified gender" but also from "self-identified *sex*." In other words, while acknowledging the attempt to define gender identity as part of sex, at the very same time, the study maintains "sex" as something that exists separate from this. This is at once a nod toward and dismissal of transness, and it demonstrates how the study makes space for the contextualities and complexities of biology while also fixing biology.

This treatment of sex is not only problematic in the context of trans politics, however. I argue that it is also not adequate for understanding sexuality, including sexual behavior. The study purports to include only people whose "biological sex" and "self-identified sex/gender" "match" (Ganna et al. 2019: 2). This means that while the authors claim to analyze same-"sex" sexual behavior, in fact, they are presumably writing about same-cisgender sexual behavior, too. But notice that this is not what is claimed. One reason this might be the case is that sexual behavior, attraction, identity, and fantasy are not easily reducible to simple sexual dimorphism. Queer archives are full of examples of this, but I'll give just one: here is Frieda, whose voice appears in the Sex Variant Study of the 1930s and whose story is recounted by Jennifer Terry (1999: 227):

> At twenty-six I found Ursula, a woman I am actually in love with. . . . She is a big, bold, mannish, fat woman who heaves into a room like a locomotive under full steam. . . . To me this force, this energy, this bigness and boldness are tremendously attractive. My admiration for bulk is such that I really enjoy getting into bed with this mountain of flesh. . . . She is 100 percent masculine, both mentally and physically.

In this passage, Frieda might be describing her experience of "same-sex sexual behavior," but how relevant is "same-sexness" to the sexual practice being described? Even though she seems to experience sex apart from gender (specifying that Ursula is "a woman," though she is "100 percent masculine"), Frieda's desire seems to be framed around masculinity and even aspects of embodiment more generally (in the form of bulk). If we were to turn to Ursula's experience, it is likely that she would describe her sexual preference differently. Would it then really make sense to describe her sexual behavior as the same as Frieda's? Quite simply, are both really practicing forms of "same-sex sexual behavior"? Is there even a sameness of sex here?

The GWAS's concept of sex as defined by biology allows for an organizing binary, even if that concept covers over the wild slipperiness and play of sex/gender within (queer) sexual practice. Such an organizing binary requires distinguishing between "sexuality" or "sexual behavior" on the one hand and "sex" on the other, such that one can have queer sexuality alongside stable, dimorphic sex. The study, much like most social, behavioral, and medical sciences, treats the distinction between these realms as self-evident, but this is a cultural and historical effect, entangled in power relations. It has been tied to a politics of respectability and homonormativity. It has also contributed to racial and class inequalities and to colonial mentalities, as well. For example, during the 1950s, many homophile groups in the United States sought to promote gender normativity among "homosexuals" as a means of gaining credibility (356). Members of the Mattachine Society pressured its left-leaning founders to "abandon their radical class politics, while simultaneously rejecting 'overtness,' 'flamboyance' and gender-transgressive markers of sexuality" (Valentine 2006: 43). In the 1980s, many lesbian feminists understood the category of "woman" as essential, which is to say determined and unchanging, but saw lesbianism as a choice: the embrace of a political ethos that rejects patriarchal heterosexuality (47). Butch-femme culture, a staple of working-class lesbian culture, was then viewed as a bad reproduction of patriarchy and anti-feminist. In each of these cases, sexuality becomes separate from sex and gender such that queer sexual practice does not interrupt the inhabitation of normative, binary sex and gender. To take one last example, many Native and Indigenous people have developed modes of self-understanding, such as two-spirit, that do not separate sex and gender from sexuality (McMullin 2011; Roen 2001). In fact, as Joanne Barker (2017: 13) explains, "Critical Indigenous studies scholars have uncovered multiple (not merely third genders or two-spirits) identificatory categories of gender and sexuality within Indigenous languages that defy binary logics and analyses. Within these categories, male, man, and masculine and female, woman, and feminine are not necessarily equated or predetermined by anatomical sex; thus, neither are social identity, desire, or pleasure." In this framework, sex is not determined by anatomy, and sex, gender, and sexuality, in their entanglement, are "reckoned in social relationships and responsibilities" (13). Thus, while it is true that the GWAS's separation of sex (as in male and female) from sexuality does not stand out from dominant Eurocentric modes of understanding, and is probably in line with the vision of the LGBTQ+ activist organizations the scientists consulted, it is worth pointing out that this distinction is not neutral or universal. It is not an essential property of the body or phenomenal experience.

This brings me, finally, to my last point: while racial typologies do not organize the study, racial logics inform the ways in which the research is communicated. In fact, the GWAS's treatment of "sex" can be read as part and parcel of what Sylvia Wynter (2003: 257) calls the "overrepresentation of 'Man.'" The

GWAS is based only on the analysis of the DNA of "participants of European ancestry" (Ganna et al. 2019: 7). In the field of genomics, the argument is that such an approach to human difference shifts from "typological notions of race to statistical notions of difference among populations" (Shim et. al. 2014: 505). Populations are understood as geographically based, produced through particular migrations and geographic dispersion, and therefore categorized by gradual variations across space rather than discrete biological types. Nonetheless, typological and geographic models often interweave with one another (Fullwiley 2008).

There may be reasons for a GWAS to focus on a particular, geographically based set of DNA samples: as a control, for reasons of internal validity, and in recognition that DNA is only meaningful within particular environments. However, in the published study and its paratexts, the limited sample is never explained; it is just recognized in passing as a limit. This naturalizes the choice, treating it as self-evident, without need for explanation. It is also notable that while the GWAS is based on "participants of European ancestry," its conclusions consistently and repeatedly remain unmarked by ancestry. For example, in the one-page published research article summary, nowhere do we see mention of this sample. The summary of the study's conclusions is posited in general, as well: "Same-sex sexual behavior is influenced by not one or a few genes but many" (Ganna et al. 2019: 1). The article's title, "Large-Scale GWAS Reveals Insights into the Genetic Architecture of Same-Sex Sexual Behavior," does nothing to alert the reader to the specificity of the sample. Both the summary article and the research article itself even begin with a specific nod to the universal: "Across human societies and in both sexes, some 2 to 10% of individuals report engaging in sex with same-sex partners" (1). White people often stand in for the universal, representative of the human while also becoming invisible as a particularity. This positioning of whiteness racializes others, who come to stand apart from the universal human. The research treats "participants of European ancestry" in the same way that whiteness is often framed. Because of this, I argue that racial logics inform how the DNA samples are represented, even if those samples are not, strictly speaking, organized according to racial typologies but rather to geographic population. It is not much of a jump then to argue that the study partakes in the "overrepresentation of Man," as the European bourgeois becomes figured as the universal (Wynter 2003: 257). "Any attempt to unsettle the coloniality of power," Wynter writes, "will call for the unsettling of this overrepresentation" (260). For Wynter, this unsettling will challenge the dominant "biocentric" model that "assumes we are, totally and completely and purely, biological beings, beholden to evolution" (McKittrick 2015: 2). This model, which finds its ascendency with Darwinian science and was "implemented by the West and by its intellectuals," has been entangled in what Wynter (2003: 263, 260) calls the "coloniality of power." That is, it is within the biocentric paradigm that we have the emergence of "race," which legitimizes inequality within liberal democracy.

It would be unfair to argue that the GWAS assumes that we are "totally and completely and purely biological beings" (McKittrick 2015: 2). However, the biocentric model appears in this study in its reliance on "sex as defined by biology" and in its assumption that the separation of "sexuality" from "sex" is neutral and obvious—a fact of biology. This treatment of "sex" connects to the GWAS's treatment of ancestry, because it is especially for a population of European ancestry that sex and sexuality are readily separable. Thus, while the GWAS makes space for the complexity and contextuality of the biology of sexuality, at the same time its understanding of "sex" returns to the biocentric model in its entanglement with the coloniality of power and its "overrepresentation of Man."

Note

All authors contributed equally and are listed alphabetically.

References

Ahmed, Sara. 2006. "The Nonperformativity of Antiracism." *Meridians: Feminism, Race, Translationalism* 7, no. 1: 104–26.

Barker, Joanne. 2017. "Introduction: Critically Sovereign." In *Critically Sovereign: Indigenous Gender, Sexuality, and Feminist Studies*, edited by Joanne Barker, 1–44. Durham, NC: Duke University Press.

Bayer, Ronald. 1981. *Homosexuality and American Psychiatry: The Politics of Diagnosis.* New York: Basic Books.

Belluck, Pam. 2019. "Many Genes Influence Same-Sex Sexuality, Not a Single 'Gay Gene." *New York Times*, August 29. https://www.nytimes.com/2019/08/29/science/gay-gene-sex.html.

Cooper, Melinda. 2008. *Life as Surplus: Biotechnology and Capitalism in the Neoliberal Era.* Seattle: University of Washington Press.

de la Cretaz, Britni. 2021. "More High Schoolers Are Gender-Diverse Than We Thought." *Them*, May 20. https://www.them.us/story/high-schooler-gender-diversity-study?fbclid=IwAR0MeNd08CsPi9CTCx513c51ON6FIppZqKATlkIZtIpNsb3fFjrXK0rKCVk.

Diamond, Lisa, and Clifford J. Rosky. 2016. "Scrutinizing Immutability: Research on Sexual Orientation and U.S. Legal Advocacy for Sexual Minorities." *Annual Review of Sex Research* 54, nos. 4–5: 363–91.

Elwell, Clare. 2018. "How 500,000 Britons Are Critical to Assessing Global Disease Risk." *Financial Times*, August 22. https://www.ft.com/content/80c82a0a-a48f-11e8 -8ecf-a7ae1beff35b.

Epstein, Steven. 1987. "Gay Politics, Ethnic Identity: The Limits of Social Construction-ism." *Socialist Review* 93/94 (May–August): 9–54.

Epstein, Steven. 2020. "The Politics of Medical Knowledge." Presentation at the Annual Meeting of the American Sociological Association, virtual conference, August 8–11.

Foucault, Michel. 1970. *The Order of Things: An Archaeology of the Human Sciences*. New York: Pantheon Books.

Fullwiley, Dana. 2008. "The Molecularization of Race." In *Revisiting Race in a Genomic Age*, edited by Barbara A. Koenig, Sandra Soo-Jin Lee, and Sarah S. Richardson, 149–71. New Brunswick, NJ: Rutgers University Press.

Gallup. 2020. "Gay and Lesbian Rights." *Gallup Historical Trends*. https://news.gallup .com/poll/1651/gay-lesbian-rights.aspx.

Ganna, Andrea, et al. 2019. "Large-Scale GWAS Reveals Insights into the Genetic Archi-tecture of Same-Sex Sexual Behavior." *Science* 365, no. 6456. https://www.science .org/doi/10.1126/science.aat7693.

Grzanka, Patrick R. 2018. "*The Straight Line: How the Fringe Science of Ex-gay Therapy Reoriented Sexuality* by Tom Waidzunas." *New Genetics and Society* 37: 268–70.

Grzanka, Patrick R. 2019. "Queer Survey Research and the Ontological Dimensions of Heterosexism." In *Imagining Queer Methods*, edited by Amin Ghaziani and Matt Brim, 84–102. New York: New York University Press.

Gurjao, Carino. 2019. "Unintended, but Not Unanticipated: The Consequences of Human Behavioral Genetics." *Broadminded Blog*, August 29. https://www.broadinstitute .org/blog/opinion-unintended-not-unanticipated-consequences-human-behavioral -genetics.

Hamer, Dean, and Peter Copeland. 1994. *The Science of Desire: The Search for the Gay Gene and the Biology of Behavior*. New York: Simon & Schuster.

Hegarty, Peter. 1997. "Materializing the Hypothalamus: A Performative Account of the 'Gay Brain.'" *Feminism & Psychology* 7, no. 3: 355–72.

Ikegawa, S. 2012. "A Short History of the Genome-Wide Association Study: Where We Were and Where We are Going." *Genomics & Informatics* 10, no. 4: 220–25.

Jones, Jeffrey M. 2021. "LGBT Identification Rises to 5.6% in Latest U.S. Estimate." Gallup, February 24. https://news.gallup.com/poll/329708/lgbt-identification-rises -latest-estimate.aspx.

Kahn, Jonathan. 2012. *Race in a Bottle: The Story of BiDil and Racialized Medicine in a Post-Genomic Age*. New York: Columbia University Press.

Karkazis, Katrina. 2019. "The Misuses of 'Biological Sex.'" *The Lancet* 394, no. 10212: 1898–99.

Kelley, Harold H. 1967. "Attribution Theory in Social Psychology." *Nebraska Symposium on Motivation* 15: 192–238.

Kendler, Kenneth S. 2019. "From Many to One to Many—The Search for Causes of Psychiatric Illness." *JAMA Psychiatry* 76, no. 10: 1085–91. https://doi.org/10.1001/jamapsychiatry.2019.1200.

Kidd, Kacie M., Gina M. Sequeira, Claudia Douglas, Taylor Paglisotti, David J. Inwards-Breland, Elizabeth Miller, and Robert W. S. Coulter. 2021. "Prevalence of Gender-Diverse Youth in an Urban School District." *Pediatrics* 147, no. 6: e2020049823. https://doi.org/10.1542/peds.2020-049823.

Marmor, Judd. 1965. *Sexual Inversion: The Multiple Roots of Homosexuality.* New York: Basic Books.

Marmor, Judd. 1980. *Homosexual Behavior: A Modern Reappraisal.* New York: Basic Books.

Marmor, Judd. 1985. "Homosexuality: Nature or Nurture." *Harvard Medical School Mental Health Letter* 5–6. Judd Marmor Papers, collection 2007–009, box 1, folder 5, ONE National Gay amd Lesbian Archives, Los Angeles.

McIntosh, Bennett. 2019. "There's (Still) No Gay Gene." *Harvard Magazine*, August. www.harvardmagazine.com/2019/08/there-s-still-no-gay-gene.

McKittrick, Katherine. 2015. *Sylvia Wynter: On Being Human as Praxis.* Durham, NC: Duke University Press.

McMullin, Dan Taulapapa. 2011. "*Fa'afafine* Notes: On Tagaloa, Jesus, and Nafanua." In *Queer Indigenous Studies: Critical Interventions in Theory, Politics, and Literature*, edited by Quo-Li Driskill, Scott Lauria Morgensen, Brian Joseph Gilley, and Chris Finley, 81–94. Tucson: University of Arizona Press.

Otis, Don. 2019. "'No One Born Gay'—Largest Study Ever Conducted Finds No Genetic Link." StephenBlack.org, September 11. https://www.stephenblack.org/blog/post/no-one-born-gay-gwas.

Panofsky, Aaron. 2014. *Misbehaving Science: Controversy and Development of Behavior Genetics.* Chicago: University of Chicago Press.

Phelps, Steven M., and Robbee Wedow. 2019. "What Genetics Is Teaching Us about Sexuality." *New York Times*, August 29. https://www.nytimes.com/2019/08/29/opinion/genetics-sexual-orientation-study.html.

Roen, Katrina. 2001. "Transgender Theory and Embodiment: The Risk of Racial Marginalization." *Journal of Gender Studies* 10, no. 3: 253–63.

Rosario, Vernon A. 2003. "An Interview with Judd Marmor, MD." *Journal of Gay and Lesbian Psychotherapy* 7, no. 4: 23–34.

Schiappa, Edward, Peter B. Gregg, and Dean E. Hewes. 2006. "Can One TV Show Make a Difference? Will and Grace and the Parasocial Contact Hypothesis." *Journal of Homosexuality* 51, no. 4: 15–37.

Shim, Janet K., Sara L. Ackerman, Katherine Weatherford Darling, Robert A. Hiatt, and Sandra Soo-Jin Lee. 2014. "Race and Ancestry in the Age of Inclusion: Technique and Meaning in Post-Genomic Science." *Journal of Health and Social Behavior* 55, no. 4: 504–18.

Shrier, Abigail. 2020. *Irreversible Damage: The Transgender Craze Seducing Our Daughters.* Washington, DC: Regnery.

Somerville, Siobhan. 1994. "Scientific Racism and the Emergence of the Homosexual Body." *Journal of the History of Sexuality* 5, no. 2: 243–66.

Sunder Rajan, Kaushik. 2006. *Biocapital: The Constitution of Postgenomic Life.* Durham, NC: Duke University Press.

Terry, Jennifer. 1999. *An American Obsession: Science, Medicine, and Homosexuality in Modern Society.* Chicago: University of Chicago Press.

Valentine, David. 2006. *Imagining Transgender: An Ethnography of a Category.* Durham, NC: Duke University Press.

Waidzunas, Tom, and Steven Epstein. 2015. "'For Men Arousal Is Orientation': Bodily Truthing, Technosexual Scripts, and the Materialization of Sexualities through the Phallometric Test." *Social Studies of Science* 45, no. 2: 187–213.

Walters, Suzanna Danuta. 2014. *The Tolerance Trap: How God, Genes, and Good Intentions are Sabotaging Gay Equality.* New York: New York University Press.

Wuest, Joanna. 2019. "The Scientific Gaze in American Transgender Politics: Contesting the Meanings of Sex, Gender, and Gender Identity in the Bathroom Rights Cases." *Politics and Gender* 15, no. 2: 336–60.

Wuest, Joanna. 2021. "From Pathology to 'Born Perfect': Science, Law, and Citizenship in American LGBTQ+ Advocacy." *Perspectives on Politics* 19, no. 3 (September): 838–53.

Wynter, Sylvia. 2003. "Unsettling the Coloniality of Being/Power/Truth/Freedom." *CR: The New Centennial Review* 3, no. 3: 257–337.

Zietsch, Brendan. 2021. "Darwinian Paradox: How Has Homosexuality Persisted During Evolution?" *SciTech Daily*, August 26. https://scitechdaily.com/darwinian-paradox-how-has-homosexuality-persisted-during-evolution/.

BLACK ECOLOGIES (HUMANITY, ANIMALITY, PROPERTY)

Jean-Thomas Tremblay

Black Gathering: Art, Ecology, Ungiven Life
Sarah Jane Cervenak
Durham, NC: Duke University Press, 2021. xii + 194 pp.

Nature's Wild: Love, Sex, and Law in the Caribbean
Andil Gosine
Durham, NC: Duke University Press, 2021. x + 178 pp.

Becoming Human: Matter and Meaning in an Antiblack World
Zakiyyah Iman Jackson
New York: New York University Press, 2020. x + 303 pp.

In *Incidents in the Life of a Slave Girl*, Harriet Jacobs ([1861] 2001) submits a zoology of the Southern US plantation and its environs. As a recent fugitive, Linda Brent (Jacobs's pseudonym) hides from her pursuers behind bushes, where she is injured by "a reptile of some kind," "something cold and slimy" (83). Days later, she and family friend Peter must wait in "Snake Swamp"; "hundreds of mosquitos . . . [poison their] flesh" as "snake after snake" crawls at their feet (94–95). "But," she insists, "even those large, venomous snakes were less dreadful to my imagination than the white men in that community called civilized" (95). For seven years, she shares an attic's crawl space with "rats and mice" as well as "hundreds of little red insects, fine as a needle's point, that [pierce] through [her] skin, and [produce] an intolerable burning" (95, 97). Even after she reaches New York, Linda fears being recognized by the Southerners "swarming" the city: "Hot weather brings out snakes and slaveholders, and I like one class of venomous creatures as little as I do the other" (143).

GLQ 29:1
DOI 10.1215/10642684-10144463
© 2023 by Duke University Press

Jacobs animalizes the slaveholder, classifying him as the most dangerous, and most evil, of "venomous creatures." In predicating a Black woman's freedom in the antebellum era on a negotiated proximity to some threatening creatures and not others, Jacobs shuffles the Enlightenment logic whereby "white men" secure their place "in that community called civilized" by exempting themselves from an animality they instead ascribe to Black and Indigenous people. I say *shuffles* because Jacobs does not collapse the human–animal hierarchy; she revises membership in each category by hinting at a notion of white animality. Jacobs's animalization of whiteness constitutes one rhetorical strategy—her condemnation of white Southerners' failure to live up to Christian values being another—meant to bring Black humanity into sharp relief. If Jacobs maintains the human's primacy and integrity, it is because her abolitionist project is embedded in a sentimental tradition. Within this tradition, readers, such as the white, Northern, Christian women whom Jacobs explicitly addresses, are invited to express sympathy toward the enslaved—to recognize, that is, their humanity.

Jacobs interferes with the legal and discursive management of Blackness's relation to nature undergirding the animalization and propertization of Black people.[1] What would such interference look like if it did not happen in the name of Black humanity, either because Black animality and humanity were more symbiotic than they appeared or because being granted humanity within a white supremacist regime were simply not desirable? Recent monographs by Sarah Jane Cervenak, Andil Gosine, and Zakiyyah Iman Jackson take up this question.

The critique of humanization in the fields dedicated to race and sexuality has generally adopted, as its unit of analysis, sentiment, emotion, affect, or feeling. Breakthrough studies have inquired into a recognition of Black humanity that "[holds] out the promise not of liberating the flesh or redeeming one's suffering but rather intensifying it" (Hartman 1997: 5); the "culture of true feeling" that tends to "elevate the ethic of personal sacrifice, suffering, and mourning over a politically 'interested' will to socially transformative action" (Berlant 2008: 35, 55); the consolidation of nineteenth-century biopower as "a sentimental mode that regulated the circulation of feeling throughout the population and delineated differential relational capacities of matter" (Schuller 2018: 7); and minoritarian practices of "unfeeling" that "signal skepticism and reluctance to signify the appropriate expressions of affect that are socially legible as human" (Yao 2021: 7). The contested terrain demarcated by Cervenak's, Gosine's, and Jackson's studies is not so much that of feeling as that of nature—specifically, the perceived and enforced contiguity to or alienation from nature of Black people and people deemed sexually deviant, two categories that overlap in the archive of coloniality.[2] I read these three books, together, as marking an ecological turn in the radical critique of humanization. Their authors enter the natural world to reencounter humanization as a process of enclosure rather than liberation, and to find fugitive ontologies and epistemologies in the shadow of the human.

The scholarship pairing Blackness and ecology in US and hemispheric contexts has proceeded along two main axes. The first concerns environmental racism, a significant configuration of environmental inequality. Dorceta E. Taylor (2014), for instance, models an environmental justice scholarship attuned to the disproportionate exposure of Black communities, communities of color, and low-income communities to environmental hazards like pollution. In the twenty-first century, such events as Hurricane Katrina (Hosbey 2018), the Flint water crisis (Pulido 2016), and the COVID-19 pandemic (Njoku 2021) have stressed the indissociability of anti-Blackness from the bio- and necropolitics of displacement, privatization, and infection.[3] The second axis tells something of an origin story about the transformations that have fossilized into the industrial, then late-industrial, landscape of environmental racism. This story's framework, the "Plantationocene," makes a prefixal adjustment to the now ubiquitous "Anthropocene," which inscribes the present in an era when human activity amounts to a geological force.[4] "The plantation," Wendy Wolford (2021: 1623) explains, "has propelled colonial exploration, sustained an elite, perpetuated a core–periphery dualism within and between countries, organized a highly racialized labor force worldwide, and shaped both the cultures we consume and the cultural norms we inhabit and perform." In trading the undifferentiated and unsituated position of *anthropos*—the human—for the plantation as birth site of a certain world order and a certain relation to the earth, Wolford and other researchers of the Plantationocene echo the insight, conveyed by Saidiya Hartman (2006), Jared Sexton (2018), Christina Sharpe (2016), and other Black studies scholars, that the Middle Passage represented nothing less than an epochal rupture.

While traces of the above inquiries, including an attention to the uneven geographies of harm and the ecological disruption of colonialism and capitalism, can be found in their books, Cervenak, Gosine, and Jackson bring distinct methods and commitments to the study of Black ecologies. Several investigations of environmental racism and the Plantationocene have taken place under the umbrella of anthropology, sociology, geography, or public health. By contrast, Cervenak, Gosine, and Jackson favor an approach not social-scientific but philosophical and aesthetic. They risk bold, overarching claims about the dominant rationality of scientific and political modernity, positing as some of its tenets the alignment of "anti-Black and anti-earth" material and discursive practices, in Cervenak's (6) case, and the traffic between Black and Indigenous humanity and animality, in Jackson's and Gosine's. Moreover, all three authors zoom in on the ways Black visual, literary, and performed arts mediate this dominant rationality. They occupy the aesthetic as a register that exacerbates the contradictions animating anti-Black norms and laws, inasmuch as the colonial common sense that would otherwise stabilize the meaning of race, sex, nature, and property—all criteria for what counts as humanity and who counts as human—is upended.

Of the three volumes foregrounded here, Jackson's *Becoming Human: Matter and Meaning in an Antiblack World* is philosophically the most ambitious. A mere two years out of the printer as of my writing this, *Becoming Human* has already secured a canonical status. Excerpts from the book previously published in article form are cited abundantly and favorably in Cervenak's *Black Gathering: Art, Ecology, Ungiven Life* (65–66) and Gosine's *Nature's Wild: Love, Sex, and Law in the Caribbean* (10). *Becoming Human* builds on the premise that Black animality is not, nor was it ever, antithetical to Black humanity. Accordingly, Jackson "[reinterprets] Enlightenment thought not as black 'exclusion' or 'denied humanity' but rather as the violent imposition and appropriation—inclusion and recognition—of black(ened) humanity in the interest of plasticizing that very humanity, whereby 'the animal' is one but not the only form blackness is thought to encompass" (3). Humanization, then, shapes the matter and meaning of Blackness in ways that may concur with animalization.[5]

In a chapter on, among other things, Toni Morrison's 1987 novel *Beloved* (also discussed in Cervenak's *Black Gathering*), Jackson reckons with the "aporia" of "[slave] humanity" (45). Her assertion that humanization was "not an antidote to slavery's violence" but "a technology for producing a *kind* of human" (46) recalls Monique Allewaert's report on the advent of alternative humanities on the plantation.[6] Yet, Jackson does not rely on a typology, like Allewaert's (2013: 85, 6), that distinguishes between the human, the animal, the object, the plant, and "the *parahuman*," the latter category designating "the slave and maroon persons who seventeenth- through nineteenth-century Anglo-European colonists typically proposed were not legally or conceptually equivalent to human beings while at the same time not being precisely inhuman." The absence from Jackson's book of such a historically informed typology is, I believe, worth noting. Whereas Allewaert's case studies revolve around documents from the seventeenth- to nineteenth-century American tropics, Jackson's, in majority though not in totality, revolve around contemporary African diasporic cultural production. That *Becoming Human* exceeds historicism in the strict sense does not mean that Jackson's claims are a- or transhistorical; they may be best labeled, like those of Plantationocene scholars, epochal.

Jackson's equation between recognizing and plasticizing Black humanity is indicative of a broad, cross-disciplinary curiosity about plasticity, "the capacity of a given body or system to generate new form, whether internally or through external intervention" (Schuller and Gill-Peterson 2020: 1). Scholars in trans, queer, Black, and race and ethnic studies have exposed plasticity's operation as "a key logic underpinning the modern notion of racial difference" and "an enlisted feature of state power" (Schuller and Gill-Peterson 2020: 2). Per Jackson's nomenclature, plasticity names "a mode of transmogrification whereby the fleshy being of blackness is experimented with as if it were infinitely malleable lexical and biological matter, such that blackness is produced as sub/super/human at once, a form where form shall not hold: potentially 'everything and nothing' at the level of ontology" (3). By this scheme, categories of race and sex owe their "world-wrecking capacities and death-dealing effects" to the modulation of the flesh's mobility and vitality (121). Against Kyla Schuller (2018), who argues that, within nineteenth-century biopolitics, Black people appeared inert, undifferentiated, and unoptimized, thus marking the constitutive outside to binary sex differentiation as civilizational achievement, Jackson insists that "the fluidification of 'life' and fleshy existence" on sites like the plantation yielded hegemonic notions of "woman," "mother," and "female body" (11). It is from the vantage point of Blackness's fluidification qua bestialization or thingification that the literary and visual artifacts compiled in *Becoming Human*—from Audre Lorde's 1980 *Cancer Journals* to Octavia E. Butler's 1984 short story "Bloodchild," to Wangechi Mutu's mid-2000s artworks—further Sylvia Wynter's (2003) project of rupturing the human.

Gosine pursues an analogous objective in a volume that blends colonial history, art criticism, and anecdotes about his upbringing in a Trinidadian Catholic all-boys school (see esp. 1–3, 12–16, 103–4). To do so, Gosine tracks, first, the introduction, throughout the expansion of European colonization in Africa, Asia, and the Americas, of "legal statutes that set out 'civil' parameters of sex, including laws forbidding interracial and homosexual sex," and, second, the disciplining of sexuality by postcolonial states since the retreat of European powers (4, 31). Gosine's search for traces of unruly bodies' animalization takes him to the narratives alleging cannibalistic practices by Indigenous peoples and the artistic responses they have elicited. Gosine demonstrates a penchant for subversive art and art criticism; his book truly lives up to its titular wild.[7] For instance, Guadeloupean artist Kelly Sinnapah Mary, whose paintings feature prominently in *Nature's Wild* and on its cover, refuses the onus of distancing colonized people from animals. Instead, she collapses that distance through representations of human–animal hybrids. Sinnapah Mary's art, as Gosine interprets it, trades the affirmation of Caribbean

humanity and its associated "politics of respectability" for a concession and a rhetorical question: "*We are animal; so what?*" (129). I decipher nothing prescriptive
in Gosine's verbalization of Sinnapah Mary's glorious nonchalance—no call, say,
to cultivate a disidentificatory (Muñoz 1999) attachment to Caribbean hybridity.
Something more pragmatic is on offer: the setup for a thought experiment that con-
sists in imagining oneself "freed from proving [oneself] *not animal*" (150).

Nature's Wild makes an important contribution to queer studies by decod-
ing the sodomy legislation implemented in the British colonies in the context of
"a general anxiety about the Pandora's box of competing norms and behaviors
potentially opened by the Europeans' metaphorical and literal penetration of 'new
worlds,' which held threatening examples of alternative versions of how humans
might live outside the patriarchal, hierarchical Christian model" (23). Criminal
codes, Gosine explains, drew clear lines between acceptable and unacceptable
sexual behavior and, by extension, between human and animal. While "animals
have sex, . . . humans have sexual cultures," he sums up, and cultures are prone
to regulation (73). In many ways, *Nature's Wild* and Christopher Chitty's (2020)
Sexual Hegemony: Statecraft, Sodomy, and Capital in the Rise of the World System
function as companion pieces. They provide, as a pair, a remarkably far-reaching
history of nonreproductive sex amid the rise and consolidation of the colonial and
capitalist order.

Becoming Human and *Black Gathering*, too, make convincing cases for
sexuality studies as an intuitive home for the study of Black ecologies. They do
so by extending a Black feminist theoretical and political lineage. When Jackson
states that "antiblackness produces differential biocultural effects of both gender
and sex" (9), for instance, we hear echo Hortense Spillers's (1987: 67, 66) claim
that the "theft of the body" enacted in the Middle Passage and its legal and discursive ripple effect has frustrated the "symbolic integrity" of male and female, patriarchy and matriarchy. Whereas Jackson evaluates slavery's impact on the sex/gender
system, Cervenak draws on a more utopian Black feminist tradition, one that sum-
mons "other 'worlds' engendered by the absence of weight and measure" (82).

Black Gathering's utopianism bespeaks an investment, inherited from
performance studies, in what artworks are as well as what they do. Cervenak
approaches Black ecologies not from the perspective of animality but from that
of property, cataloging the ways Black artists and writers have "aestheticized and
poeticized a relation between togetherness and ungivable living," or life that is not,
and cannot be, subsumed into property relations (3). She opens the book with an
attentive account of the African American visual artist Xaviera Simmons's *Harvest,*

a 2010 installation made of 231 wood panels on which are painted various words and phrases (1–4). In *Harvest*, Cervenak observes, "[social] life . . . orbits into and out of view as verbs disappear and reappear from and without their proper subjects and half-indicated socialities bloom as an earth without enclosure" (3). The installation's "deregulated togetherness" eschews a model of Black freedom as "propertied self-possession" to conjure a life that is not "given over to propertied regulation and inscription" (1, 6, 7). Art, for Cervenak, generates a commons of sorts: it holds space for Black life, unenclosed.

What most fundamentally distinguishes *Black Gathering* from *Becoming Human* and *Nature's Wild* is the external position its author occupies relative to the communities she addresses. As someone who, like me, "benefits from whiteness," Cervenak is after an abolitionist engagement with Black studies, one whose interpretive strategies do not reproduce "the very propertizing and extraction otherwise critiqued" (11). The key to such an engagement, as she sees it, is to refrain, in chapters on such works as Gayl Jones's experimental writings and Leonardo Drew's sculptures, from "attempting some false analytic resolution of Black gatherings' indeterminate meanings and ambulation" (11). I notice in this engagement an anti-sentimental stance: a refusal to make the white gaze the guarantor of Black expression's meaning.

At the same time, I wonder whether Jackson would warn of a threat of fluidification. Is it indeed possible to shield the material and semiotic flux that guarantees Blackness's ungivability from the flux that denotes its plasticity? The juxtaposition of Cervenak's, Gosine's, and Jackson's books thus locates, at the heart of Black ecologies, the question of which indeterminacies and hybridities are desirable and which are not—which activate imaginaries of liberation and which are tethered to apparatuses of capture.

I end as I began: with an aesthetic vignette, and one set in New York City, where Jacobs found freedom. The vignette's focus, Tourmaline's short film *Atlantic Is a Sea of Bones* (2017), occupies a tension I have associated with Black ecologies between two modes of fluidification: the first functioning as a *dispositif* of capture (slavery and its afterlives, such as segregation, incarceration, and policing), and the second encompassing fugitive practices (aesthetic and social forms that induce glitches in the logic of propertization). *Atlantic Is a Sea of Bones* inhabits aquatic ecologies on multiple scales. One ecology is domestic: cast members plunge into and arise from a bathtub filled with water or milk in gestures of cleansing and rebirth. Another is fluvial: the Hudson River, into which the bathwater may be discharged, is home to Manhattan's West Side Piers, where trans and queer people congregated en masse in the 1970s and 1980s. Yet another is marine: the Hudson drains into the Atlantic Ocean, across which enslaved people were forcibly transported and, as the film's title reminds us, into which some were thrown during the Middle Passage.

Tourmaline's film begins at the Whitney Museum of American Art, which in 2015 moved into a Renzo Piano–designed building with floor-to-ceiling windows overlooking the piers. Ballroom legend Egyptt LaBeija enjoys the elevated viewpoint and reminisces, "I literally lived on that pier that's no longer there. I lived there, in a hut. I lived on there, and I slept on this thing right under there, because I was homeless. I had to make money, and I had nowhere to go. And then one day, I just snapped out. I said, 'This can't work no more.' And I started reaching for better things. Oh my god! I've never seen it from this angle before, so, it's a lot. I don't want to cry. Well, I can cry now, I don't got no make-up on." LaBeija lets out a bittersweet giggle and pauses before solemnly announcing, "The times of the Village, from 14th Street to Christopher Street. The memories. People should never forget where they came from."

Geo Wyeth's electronic score guides us through a surrealist sequence: LaBeija, Jamal Lewis, and other performers walk, dance, and pose in sets saturated by ultraviolet light. The sequence relays *Afro-fabulations*, Tavia Nyong'o's (2018: 1–5) term for queer practices of speculation that rearrange Black time and temporality.[8] Multi-scalar ecological dwelling in *Atlantic Is a Sea of Bones* reactivates Black trans and queer pasts that resist idealization—"This can't work no more," LaBeija remembers thinking of life on the pier—but culminate in a present that is not that of a corporate museum situated at the edge of a gentrified West Village where Black trans and queer life has been policed out of existence. The closing shot features a femme-presenting individual dressed in a red sequined gown. The performer stands on a balcony, their back to the camera and their face to the Hudson, and strikes a pose (fig. 1). A magic trick has been performed. The Whitney now out of frame, the elevated viewpoint that so fascinated LaBeija is salvaged from institutionality. The vanishing of the museum as arbiter of art and humanity, American or otherwise, makes room for something new, or old. Something else. By raising their hand, the performer raises the dead: life returns to the pier, its enduring stilts now looking like a bustling crowd reborn and gathered.

Somewhere between Jackson's, Gosine's, and Cervenak's Black ecologies, *Atlantic Is a Sea of Bones* exemplifies a speculative, though not romanticizing, relation to indeterminacies and hybridities. In Tourmaline's film, histories of enslavement are intercut with performances of rebirth out of bondage, and histories of housing insecurity with performances of property abolition. Fluidification,

Figure 1. Still from Tourmaline's *Atlantic Is a Sea of Bones* (2017).

as a locus of aesthetic experimentation, accommodates neither strictly a chronology of capture nor one of liberation; it instead points to the traffic between these processes, their ecological copresence.

Notes

1. Statements about "never [dreaming about being] a piece of merchandise" as an enslaved child and the "dream" of a then-free Linda to "sit with [her] children in a home of [her] own" bookend the narrative (Jacobs [1861] 2001: 8, 164).
2. Schuller (2018: 3), who stresses "[sentimentalism's] organic nature," bridges the gap between feeling and nature in critiques of humanization.
3. For a survey of racial ecologies of harm, see Nishime and Hester Williams 2018. For early returns on a long-term, collective project on "Black ecologies" intended "to collect historical and contemporary narratives from Black communities that offer alternative epistemic entry points for historicizing and interrupting mounting ecological crisis," see Roane and Hosbey 2019.
4. On the Plantationocene, the Anthropocene, and such correlates as the Capitalocene and the Chthulucene, see Haraway 2015; Haraway et al. 2016.
5. "Recognition of personhood and humanity," specifies Jackson, "does not annul the animalization of blackness. Rather, it reconfigures discourses that have historically bestialized blackness" (18).
6. On the "all-too-fraught proximity between the enslaved black person and the nonhuman animal," see also Bennett 2020: 1.

7. On the wild as colonial rubric and queer aesthetics, see Halberstam 2020: 6–7.
8. Nyong'o (2018) offers this definition in the context of an account of the 1968 documentary *The Queen* that centers Crystal LaBeija, who would go on to cofound the House of LaBeija, Egyptt's drag family.

References

Allewaert, Monique. 2013. *Ariel's Ecology: Plantations, Personhood, and Colonialism in the American Tropics.* Minneapolis: University of Minnesota Press.

Atlantic Is a Sea of Bones. 2017. Directed by Tourmaline. New York: Visual AIDS.

Bennett, Joshua. 2020. *Being Property Once Myself: Blackness and the End of Man.* Cambridge, MA: Harvard University Press.

Berlant, Lauren. 2008. *The Female Complaint: The Unfinished Business of Sentimentality in American Culture.* Durham, NC: Duke University Press.

Chitty, Christopher. 2020. *Sexual Hegemony: Statecraft, Sodomy, and Capital in the Rise of the World System.* Durham, NC: Duke University Press.

Halberstam, Jack. 2020. *Wild Things: The Disorder of Desire.* Durham, NC: Duke University Press.

Haraway, Donna. 2015. "Anthropocene, Capitalocene, Plantationocene, Chthulucene: Making Kin." *Environmental Humanities* 6, no. 1: 159–65.

Haraway, Donna, Noboru Ishikawa, Scott F. Gilbert, Kenneth Olwig, Anna L. Tsing, and Nils Bubandt. 2016. "Anthropologists Are Talking–About the Anthropocene." *Ethnos* 81, no. 3: 535–64.

Hartman, Saidiya. 1997. *Scenes of Subjection: Terror, Slavery, and Self-Making in Nineteenth-Century America.* New York: Oxford University Press.

Hartman, Saidiya. 2006. *Lose Your Mother: A Journey Along the Atlantic Slave Trade.* New York: Farrar, Straus and Giroux.

Hosbey, Justin. 2018. "Refusing Unliveable Destinies: Toward a Future for Black Life in New Orleans." *Fire!!!* 5, no. 1: 35–47.

Jacobs, Harriet. 1861 (2001). *Incidents in the Life of a Slave Girl*, edited by Joslyn T. Pine. Mineola, NC: Dover.

Muñoz, José Esteban. 1999. *Disidentifications: Queers of Color and the Performance of Politics.* Minneapolis: University of Minnesota Press.

Nishime, Leilani, and Kim D. Hester Williams. 2018. *Racial Ecologies.* Seattle: University of Washington Press.

Njoku, Anuli U. 2021. "COVID-19 and Environmental Racism: Challenges and Recommendations." *European Journal of Environmental and Public Health* 5, no. 2: 1–9.

Nyong'o, Tavia. 2018. *Afro-Fabulations: The Queer Drama of Black Life.* New York: New York University Press.

Pulido, Laura. 2016. "Flint, Environmental Racism, and Racial Capitalism." *Capitalism Nature Socialism* 27, no. 3: 1–16.

Roane, J. T., and Justin Hosbey. 2019. "Mapping Black Ecologies." *Current Research in Digital History* 2. August 23. https://doi.org/10.31835/crdh.2019.05.

Schuller, Kyla. 2018. *The Biopolitics of Feeling: Race, Sex, and Science in the Nineteenth Century.* Durham, NC: Duke University Press.

Schuller, Kyla, and Jules Gill-Peterson. 2020. "Introduction: Race, the State, and the Malleable Body." *Social Text* 30, no. 2: 1–17.

Sexton, Jared. 2018. *Black Men, Black Feminism: Lucifer's Nocturne.* Cham, Switzerland: Palgrave Macmillan.

Sharpe, Christina. 2016. *In the Wake: On Blackness and Being.* Durham, NC: Duke University Press.

Spillers, Hortense. 1987. "Mama's Baby, Papa's Maybe: An American Grammar Book." *Diacritics* 17, no. 2: 64–81.

Taylor, Dorceta E. 2014. *Toxic Communities: Environmental Racism, Industrial Pollution, and Residential Mobility.* New York: New York University Press.

Wolford, Wendy. 2021. "The Plantationocene: A Lusotropical Contribution to the Theory." *Annals of the American Association of Geographers* 111, no. 6: 1622–39.

Wynter, Sylvia. 2003. "Unsettling the Coloniality of Being/Power/Truth/Freedom: Towards the Human, After Man, Its Overrepresentation—An Argument." *CR: The New Centennial Review*, 3, no. 3: 257–337.

Yao, Xine. 2021. *Disaffected: The Cultural Politics of Unfeeling in Nineteenth-Century America.* Durham, NC: Duke University Press.

Books in Brief

QUEER SEX AND THE CRISIS OF CAPITAL

Heather Berg

*Sexual Hegemony: Statecraft, Sodomy, and Capital in the Rise
of the World System*
Christopher Chitty, ed. Max Fox
Durham, NC: Duke University Press, 2020. xii + 225 pp.

Sexuality is not a space protected from the tedium and violence of life under capitalism, argues Christopher Chitty, and neither is it the product of capital's top-down maneuvering. Instead, it is a terrain of class conflict. Chitty's sprawling *Sexual Hegemony: Statecraft, Sodomy, and Capital in the Rise of the World System* takes us from early modern Florence to the postwar United States to tell a story about how capital flows shape sex and how, in turn, sex powers the crises of capital. "Alternate or queer sexualities," Chitty writes, "historically emerged along the fault lines of transformed property relations" (178–79). A sophisticated and daring text in queer Marxist thought, *Sexual Hegemony* refuses the artificial choice between Karl Marx and Michel Foucault, the material and the discursive. Made possible by Max Fox's careful editing of the late Chitty's unfinished dissertation, *Sexual Hegemony* is the product of a comradeship and queer care that mirrors the book's politics.

Among *Sexual Hegemony*'s most striking interventions is Chitty's insistence (one supported by a rich historical archive) that heterosexism is a tool of class struggle rather than a prejudice rooted in morality or religion. Queer sex is, sometimes, a material problem for the capitalist state. Classes weaponize the hetero family (and the straight sex that props it up) in uneven ways—Chitty convincingly writes against any sort of progress narrative—and this has little to do

GLQ 29:1

with what they really believe about good sex. *Sexual Hegemony* invites us to think about bourgeois morality not as morality that happens to be bourgeois, but as a slippery normative structure that helps create the conditions for bourgeois life (and, yes, hegemony).

Neither is the weaponization of sexuality only something that comes from the top down. The working and ruling classes have made use of sexuality as a tool of class struggle, but sexual hegemony's specifically bourgeois character comes from its force as a weapon against both ruling- and working-class antagonists. Chitty's discussion of sodomy policing in early modern Florence shows how sexual policing both served the ends of controlling working-class access to public space and "provided a pressure valve" for critiques of nobles' unchecked power (66). Later, Chitty takes us to the French Revolution and to the bourgeoisie's use of "scandals of appetite" to claim class power. The bourgeoisie turned to a scientific discourse on same-sex sex to rationalize its struggle against the excesses of the ruling class and authorize its role in reigning in the unruly publicness of the lower class. Throughout, Chitty shows a historical trend in which the working class bears the harshest costs of moralism. Ruling-class libertines emerge embarrassed but with the basic structures of class power intact.

Moving to the turn of the twentieth century, Chitty tells a story of how the working class's growing access to middle-class respectability brought about a democratization of bourgeois sexual morality: "Socioeconomic progress is directly to blame for a wider basis for sexual repression" (136). Here, Chitty is not explicitly engaged with leftist feminist writing on family abolition, but his interventions remind readers that the family was never for working-class class people in the first place. Readers of contemporary politics will see sexual moralism's uneven force in the ways bourgeois critiques of ruling-class sexual consumption get quickly turned against the working-class others who labor in sex markets, as when football magnate Robert Kraft escaped solicitation charges while the migrant sex workers he patronized did not. Chitty's history is also an education in tactics for the now.

Sexual Hegemony's focus is on European queer masculinities, and one casualty of its incompleteness is a lost opportunity to engage queer of color and feminist critique. Still, its interest in the unruly solidarities among sexual outsiders positions the text in broader conversation with thinkers ranging from Cathy Cohen to Silvia Federici, who share a commitment to a materialist analysis of sex that builds anti-capitalist solidarities. If, as for Chitty, the normal is a "status" that confers material advantages on those who can access it, to be queer is to lack that status. "Rather than marking a utopian opening up of . . . logics for self-transformative play," queerness signals the material realities of life outside the institutions of hetero capitalism (26). This method, what Chitty calls "queer realism," beckons a queerness that is both grounded and expansive.

Throughout *Sexual Hegemony*, we find queer men and poor women who have the wrong kinds of sex connected in the threats they pose to the status quo. That part of same-sex sex's disruptive force comes from its capacity to bring people together across class, race, and national lines links it to sexual labor, another space where "stranger intimacy" troubles social segmentation. *Sexual Hegemony* figures queer sex itself as a sometimes practice of solidarity. Chapter 3 introduces us to the seventeenth- and eighteenth-century sailors whose "'dirty passions' across lines of class and race" threatened solidarities that undermined not only the governance of ships but also the entire project of chattel slavery (101). *Sexual Hegemony* takes no easy guesses at the shape future sexual solidarities will take. Instead, it offers a usable past that helps us think better about what it might look like to build them.

In his introduction, Christopher Nealon notes Chitty's agnosticism about what sexual futures will or should look like. This agnosticism runs throughout the text, posing one of the book's most striking confrontations with queer studies. Chitty refuses to narrate a queerness that sits outside capitalist social relations, telling a queer history that resists both the politics of respectability and the discourse of queer alterity typically offered as its anecdote. To release attachments to queerness as alterity—its "purely negative relation to some law or norm"—is to "ask instead about the transformative and emancipatory possibilities of love and intimacy outside the institutions of the family, state, and couple form" (145). How to pursue a queerness that actively, materially, antagonizes the property relation? In the best sprit of queer anti-capitalist scholarship, Chitty makes us want to try.

Heather Berg is assistant professor in the Department of Women, Gender, and Sexuality Studies at Washington University in St. Louis.

DOI 10.1215/10642684-10144477

TRAP/TROPE: GALARTE'S TRANS-FIGURATIVE, RACIALIZED READINGS

Christina A. León

Brown Trans Figurations: Rethinking Race, Gender, and Sexuality in Chicanx/Latinx Studies
Francisco J. Galarte
Austin: University of Texas Press, 2021. viii + 192 pp.

At a moment when racialized and gendered terms are under considerable pressure, Francisco J. Galarte's *Brown Trans Figurations: Rethinking Race, Gender, and Sexuality in Chicanx/Latinx Studies* asks us to think under and with this pressure through the register of figuration. Galarte's reading of the figurative takes inspiration from Emma Pérez's (1999: 8) provocation, in a revision of Hayden White, that Chicana/o historians have been "captives of tropological interpretation." This tropological capture reflects and refracts more concertedly when considered with the additional rhetorical strictures facing Chicanx trans folks—narratological pressures that have, historically, policed access to gender affirming treatment and resources. Galarte writes with the ethos of Eva Hayward's (2017) claim that universalist narratives entail "an investment in nameable identity over and against the precarity of subjectivity" (Hayward quoted on 14). The larger task and accomplishment of *Brown Trans Figurations* is to question the figuration in these namings, which means attending to narratives of loss and relation over the identifiable claims that find solace in comfortable nominalization.

Rather than making brown trans folks the ultimate object of study, Galarte's approach looks at larger structures and histories of race, gender, and sexuality in order to resist and complicate progress narratives around the trans tipping point. The first part of the book concentrates on Chicana trans women whose deaths became a symbolic front for LGBT movements that seek legislation against hate crimes as *the* form of protection against transphobic violence. But Galarte's careful readings of the cases of Gwen Araujo and Angie Zapata, trans women murdered in 2002 and 2008, respectively, tell a more pernicious story about how trans protection can be entangled with anti-migrant/nativist policing such that the trans women become figured, in their afterlives, through tropes of trans panic, deceitful trespasser, and the hateful other. By reading the "dolorous proximity" of race and transsexuality in the Gwen Araujo case, Galarte expands on Talia Bettcher's (2007) readings of trans women figured as always already deceitful by enfolding that discourse into the extant critique of betrayal in Chicana feminism. Galarte shows, through readings of documentary film and news media alike, how such deceptive tropological entrapment becomes underscored by racist attitudes toward Chicana women more broadly—through hypervisibility read as excessive sexuality or through the Malinche trope.

Extending this dolorous reading to a trans woman inspired by Araujo, the second chapter looks to the LGBT legal battle cry to convict Angie Zapata's killer, Allen Andrade, as a hate crime. The supposed justice, for LGBT folks, served at his conviction leads Galarte to read how the trial put both Andrade and Zapata under scrutiny and how both bodies endured a maelstrom of tropes likening them to racialized, sexualized others, which ultimately served a white supremacist police state. At no point does Galarte exonerate Andrade, but he brings to the fore the attendant structural and material scaffolding of the case in ways that muddy moral outrage and complicate rights-based discourse. This relational matrix takes trans lives outside of exceptional discourse and shows how they are stitched, like the paño art that appears throughout the text, into figurations of their own making while navigating tropological impositions. Such an entangled reading practice extends devastatingly back into the Zapata family after Angie Zapata's death, as two of her siblings suffered, too, from the "overkill" of racial capitalism—one was killed in a drunk driving accident and another hospitalized in a hit-and-run crash motivated by homophobia. Galarte articulates the larger violence of the specific figurations of hypervisible lives, both trans and brown, that become obscured by regimes of power and rights-based discourse.

The second part of the book shifts to consider a different genealogy across the brown trans binary, looking to intramural gender debates in Chicana feminism between butches and FTM Chicano/x men. This necessarily centers what Galarte calls the trans/FTM "border wars" to redouble a commitment to borderlands thinking within one of the foundational thinkers of Chicana feminism, Cherríe Moraga. Rather than quickly dismissing and castigating Moraga's transphobia in "Keeping Queer Queer," Galarte rereads her attachments and border policing as itself about a feeling of possible loss: loss of a queer and a brown nation. We may ask ourselves, furthered by this trenchant critique, if political alliances need nations at all, given how national borders have been particularly fraught zones for Black and brown trans bodies. But it is also to read the borderlands, and not border logic, back into the project of an expansive Chicana feminism that needn't pathologize

Chicano/x trans men as whitened traitors, because "to conceive of the borderlands, as Anzaldúa asks us to, is to embrace the uncertain and the unknown that mark brown transfiguration" (105). Reading figurations of trans embodiment in Carla Trujillo's 2003 novel *What Night Brings* that do not exactly end in a telos of transition, Galarte considers how transfigurations have been operable, despite gendered borders upheld by Chicana feminists. Galarte achieves this task precisely by "muddying the line," or border, drawn between FTM, butch, and cis Chicana/o/x and Latina/o/x masculinities (105). This muddied line then takes us back to FTM negotiations of Chicanx community, in the fourth chapter, through a masculinity transfigured by the "cut" of trans—reading a sexology case; a documentary on FTM and Butch folks in the Bay Area, *Mind if I Call You Sir?*; and a photo of FTM and butch Chicanx masculine folks who transfigure Chicanx masculinity.

Finally, turning back to the question of gender, language, and Latinx studies, Galarte's coda "reads with the x." This entails reading the x of Latinx figuratively for what it might do to gender binaries and what it might expose about dualistic logics. Reading with the x stays in this mercurial space, bringing the book to a looping configuration that places portraits of a difficult to name model, Jim/Jaime/Ariana Aguilar, as defiantly poised and untranslatable into a stable binary gender. This insistent indeterminacy functions as a modality of reading for the x beyond the binary. Galarte's hermeneutics and the larger tapestry of the book ask that we read, yet again, the figuration of race, gender, and sexuality in recursive stride.

What can be thought together as open ended, multiple, and unfolding in a dual sense of mattering—both embodying/materializing and affectively moving (whether through pain, recognition, or both)—can also harden into a logic of capture, nominalization, and reification. This, it seems, is the charge that brown transfiguration leaves us with: reading that which cannot but be read as a risk of signification and that which requires recursive reading to unfurl border wars, to consider the aftermath of trans death, and to keep reading at the interstice of race and gender, especially now when the conservative, fascistic, right-wing energies turn over whether what is under fire is trans lives or critical race theory. The turn, though, is the move that may trap or may open, and so we are left with the charge of thinking through how tropological movements of race and gender un/settle in the various archives of racialized, gendered difference.

Christina A. León is an assistant professor in the Department of English at Princeton University.

References

Bettcher, Talia Mae. 2007. "Evil Deceivers and Make-Believers: On Transphobic Violence and the Politics of Illusion." *Hypatia* 22, no. 3: 43–65.

Hayward, Eva. 2017. "Spiderwomen." *Trap Door: Trans Cultural Production and the Politics of Visibility*, edited by Tourmaline, Eric A. Stanley, and Johanna Burton, 255–80. Cambridge, MA: MIT Press.

Pérez, Emma. 1999. *The Decolonial Imaginary: Writing Chicanas into History*. Bloomington: Indiana University Press.

DOI 10.1215/10642684-10144491

EVIL AND COMPLICATED QUEERS THROUGH HISTORY

Lee Mandelo

Bad Gays: A Homosexual History
Huw Lemmey and Ben Miller
New York: Verso, 2022. 368 pp.

In *Bad Gays: A Homosexual History*, Huw Lemmey and Ben Miller investigate "the evolution and failure of white male homosexuality" as both an "identity and a political project" (5), by telling the (his)stories of fourteen bad gays from Hellenistic emperor Hadrian to Far Right Dutch politician Pim Fortuyn. Drawing materials in part from their long-running podcast, Lemmey and Miller engage in a process of recontextualization as opposed to one of queer hagiography, or even of recovery to fill the historical record. By orienting their stories around the creation of the "homosexual" as a contingent identity, Lemmey and Miller productively reframe these queer figures as both products of and participants in the continuous project of Western empire. Rather than telling stories *of* queer history, *Bad Gays* tells stories of queers *in* history—sometimes for the better, but as one anticipates from the title, mostly for the worse.

Primarily aimed toward a general audience, *Bad Gays* explores its themes "not through scholarly argument, but [instead] through storytelling" (6)—producing a cohesive, collective argument from interconnected, individual vignettes. However, the authors cleverly and smoothly integrate scholarship from Michel Foucault, Ann Stoler, C. Riley Snorton, Jasbir Puar, Silvia Federici, Jules Gill-Peterson, and more throughout. Their citational practice, which leans on paraphrasing and endnotes, allows uninterrupted narrative flow for the casual reader (or, introductory-course student) without eliding necessary references. Chapters are arranged in rough chronological order and center largely on Europeans whose historical roles otherwise appear settled, such as Frederick the Great, Roger Casement, and Lawrence of Arabia. Within the second half of the text, the authors also explore figures from the "empire whose refusal to acknowledge itself as such is a central part of its myth: the United States" (188), including Margaret Mead, J. Edgar Hoover, and Roy Cohn. Additionally, tracing links between gay hypermasculinity and right-wing nationalism, the authors include the story of Yukio Mishima.

　　While the book is delightfully catty, occasionally salacious, and eminently readable, the homosexual histories gathered within nevertheless arise from and radiate a deep political frustration. The failures of homosexuality Lemmey and Miller explore are failures of solidarity, failures to enact broader queer liberation in favor of rights-based assimilation into the "burning house" of the hegemonic order (5). In the introduction, the authors draw three general trends from the stories: "separation from and fear of gender non-conformity, . . . appropriation of the bodies and sexualities of racialized people and denial of those people's full humanity, . . . [and an] incessant focus on the bourgeois project of 'sexuality' itself" (5). Suggesting that our understandings of queer history should derive as much from the wealthy, conservative "embodiment of evil twink energy" Lord Alfred Douglas ("Bosie") as they do from his lover Oscar Wilde, *Bad Gays* asks why contemporary queers choose to remember some ancestors and forget others—as well as what the (classed, raced, gendered, colonial) politics of that forgetting are.

　　Bad Gays' main strength therefore lies in its weaving-through of approachable, grounded critiques of colonialism, Western empire, and capitalism, as well as anthropology and sexology. Through the use of queer(ing) recontextualizations, Lemmey and Miller demonstrate how "symbolic events [often stand in] for the culmination of long-developing historical processes and the beginning of new cycles" (39). The text deftly communicates scholarly approaches to historical time and cultural critique, for example in its traceries of how the development of capitalism helped craft the circumstances for both the discovery of the "homosexual" and the rapid expansion of colonialism. Relatedly, *Bad Gays* also aims to complicate "the idea of an unchanging thread of homosexuality that passes through history" (38), buoyed along by Western cultural progress toward tolerance—a goal to which ending on the gay, Islamophobic, anti-immigrant Fortuyn lends itself.

However, the cohesion of the text's final third is looser. While the trajectories Lemmey and Miller follow post-1945 align with preceding critiques of masculinist fascism, white supremacy, and class-based exploitation, the leaps from Cohn, to Mishima, to Ronnie Kray, to Fortuyn occur rather abruptly. Though I acknowledge the limitations of trade print format, *Bad Gays'* ending arguments could have struck a more forceful note with the inclusion of perhaps three or four additional narratives. Further contextualization for the HIV/AIDS crisis, marriage and military service as "gay rights" campaigns, or the rise of neoliberalism—as opposed to compressing those critiques together—might have provided a smoother landing for the text as a whole.

Overall, though, Lemmey and Miller have constructed a solid critical text for a general audience—which also affords them opportunities for directness in their political anger and their queer humor. Of Roger Casement, the authors state, his acts of resistance "puts the lie to the idea that imperialist racism went unopposed in its day, a lie that serves to whitewash the reputation of racists like the politician and mining baron Cecil Rhodes" (123). These unflinching assessments aren't limited to colonialism; the chapter on architect Philip Johnson practically vibrates with loathing for his fascist classism. And of course, the second pleasure of *Bad Gays* is Lemmey and Miller's raucous sense of humor. In the discussion of James VI's system of patronage, for instance, they write: "There is power in being the king who sits upon the throne, but sometimes there is more power in being the throne on whom the king sits" (70). Or, consider an aside from the chapter on the gay Nazis of Weimar Berlin, which critiques erotic attachments to fascist masculinity: "(Remember that when writing your Grindr profile!)" (151).

Bad Gays: A Homosexual History ultimately concludes on a call for us, fractious queer community(s), to engage *being together* toward a queer futurity—arguing that only solidarity and alliance make liberation possible. Using the preceding stories "full of racism and exclusion" (304) as contrary examples, the text instead espouses queerness as theorized by scholars like Roderick Ferguson and writers like Larry Mitchell. By emphasizing an understanding of "how people have made and been made by history, how and why they have failed, and why we might succeed" (308), Lemmey and Miller demonstrate the potential of *Bad Gays* to offer an engaging set of stories for a broader readership—stories that provide a nuanced understanding of the past that remains with us, as well as lessons for "the revolutions of the queer future" (309).

Lee Mandelo is a doctoral candidate in gender and women's studies at the University of Kentucky.

DOI 10.1215/10642684-10144505

THE CARE PRAXIS WITHIN

Beans Velocci

Trans Care
Hil Malatino
Minneapolis: University of Minnesota Press, 2020. viii + 79 pp.

I wanted *Trans Care* to be longer. The book is what I believe reviewers typically mean when they refer to a "slim volume," coming in at—in the edition kindly sent to me by *GLQ*—seventy-nine pages, bibliography included. As a historian, I found this jarring. As a trans person refreshing Twitter to see what fresh hell is being unleashed in state legislatures today, I felt a deep sense of relief and perhaps, if you will, of being cared for. It was a feeling I wanted more of, even amid my gratitude for not having to claw my way through a four-hundred-pager while dealing with (*gestures broadly*) all of this. I dwell on this not for the sake of saying *this is a short book* but to emphasize how effectively Hil Malatino has woven form and function: reading *Trans Care* feels like an act of receiving trans care, in that it is both a balm and a reminder of the vast amount of work we still collectively need to do.

The main takeaway is this: trans care is what trans people do to make room for each other to live in a world where the institutional and familial forms of care that are supposed to sustain us often don't. Also, trans care is difficult, exhausting, real labor that is compensated only insofar as we all, in some way or another, rely on it for survival. There is no utopic or romanticized vision of care, here. "None of these struggles," Malatino writes, referring to examples like demanding lines on official paperwork for chosen names, suing health insurance companies for coverage, and pushing for the use of digital systems that allow gender changes, "are

particularly sexy" (41). Nor are they perfect. Many people are left out, overly bur-
dened, or otherwise find care itself a source of further pain. And yet, the work
must continue; it's certainly not coming from anyone else.

Five chapters take the reader on a whirlwind tour. Malatino theorizes, in
succession, the possibility of trans care to decenter cisheteronormative domestic-
ity in thinking about care labor; the inadequacy of "burnout" as a framing for
the exhaustion that adheres to that care; care work as solidarity and recognition
rather than debt and exchange; finding sustenance in archives of past trans life;
and intra-community trans practices in the wake of medical denials of care. The
book moves deftly between source material, ranging from a riff on a Fall Out Boy
t-shirt, to a close reading of pro-trans billboards, to a haunting discussion of the
letters from trans people fruitlessly seeking medical transition that are housed
in the Harry Benjamin International Gender Dysphoria Association (HBIGDA)
collection at the Kinsey Institute. Malatino's wry attention to detail weaves this
together into a constant reminder that the stuff of trans care is everywhere.

I am, without reservation, convinced. Yet, despite knowing how stodgy this
sounds, I also found myself searching for a *what next*. At one point, Malatino refers
to a photo of French photographer Claude Cahun—which they read as an ambigu-
ously gendered invitation for desire—as "a gift that I'm still figuring out how to
use" (54). This book, too, feels like a gift I am still figuring out how to use. I am
very willing to write this reaction off as a disciplinary quibble, and look forward to
conversations about where Malatino's insights get us beyond the limits of confining
things like historical method. But because of the brief length of the book, I was
more tantalized than satisfied. The chapter "Something Other than Trancestors:
Hirstory Lessons," for example, makes a compelling case for rethinking contemporary relations to trans archives. Rather than searching for clear lineages of people
just like us, which impose coercive subjectivities onto historical actors who have
already had their fair share of that by dint of living in the world as trans (or trans-
adjacent) people, Malatino suggests, we must "admit" that "there are unknowable
dimensions to our entanglements" (59). I'm so here for that. It's an open question
in trans history that requires ongoing grappling beyond Foucault-tinged categori-
cal precision or searching for recognizable trans actors in the past. But what does
that alternate relation-building look like in action? It is not immediately clear from
Trans Care. "Care praxis is always within and beyond," Malatino concludes, and
it's true. Also, I would like for us to inch closer to something instead of forever
grasping.

This leads me to another both/and consideration. There is a certain thrill-
ing ingroupiness to the text: a snarking rephrase of Foucault on Bentham that you'll

know if you know; the laughably technophilic name of a TSA-approved body scan-ner mentioned without explanation; a fly-by gloss of natureculture, "My Words to Victor Frankenstein," and Barad. I'm in on it, so I chuckled each time, impressed by the way Malatino doesn't cater to anyone demanding legibility. I'm not sure how it lands if you're not precisely the trans academic audience it's pitched for, and I'm not sure it matters. This isn't a critique of inaccessibility, though I'll be honest, *Trans Care* doesn't strike me as the kind of text I'd assign to undergrads outside of a trans studies seminar, which is a fine kind of book to be but perhaps worth a note on likely uses. Rather, it's welcome inspiration to reflect on my own efforts to drag cis readers kicking and screaming into the trans worlds they often struggle to comprehend, and I appreciate Malatino's mode as a complementary approach. Still, I remain caught between wonder and practicality, dazzled by Malatino's craft in getting a reader to occupy contradictory affects.

Trans Care is a beautiful provocation that invites readers into a "dual movement" (70) of critiquing care relations even as we rely on them. Malatino has fully succeeded: I emerged from my encounter with the text feeling simultaneously grateful and expectant, delighted and ultimately jaded. If you want to sit with your own desires for practicable solutions even as you know how the instrumentalization of that demand works, and I think you should, this is a book for you.

Beans Velocci is assistant professor in the Department of History and Sociology of Science and Program in Gender, Sexuality, and Women's Studies at the University of Pennsylvania.

DOI 10.1215/10642684-10144519

About the Contributors

Kadji Amin is associate professor of women's, gender, and sexuality studies at Emory University. He is the recipient of a Mellon Postdoctoral Fellowship in Sex from the University of Pennsylvania and a Humanities Institute Faculty Fellowship from Stony Brook University. His book, *Disturbing Attachments*: *Genet, Modern Pederasty, and Queer History* (2017), won an honorable mention for best book in LGBT studies from the GL/Q Caucus of the Modern Language Association. He is currently at work on a second book, "Trans Materialism without Gender Identity."

Howard Chiang is associate professor of history at the University of California, Davis, and past chair of the Society of Sinophone Studies. He is the author of *Transtopia in the Sinophone Pacific* (2021), a Lambda Literary Award Finalist, and *After Eunuchs: Science, Medicine, and the Transformation of Sex in Modern China* (2018), which received the International Convention of Asia Scholars Humanities Book Prize. Both books won the Bonnie and Vern L. Bullough Book Award from the Society for the Scientific Study of Sexuality. He is currently writing a book on the history of psychoanalysis and transcultural reasoning across the Pacific.

Stephanie D. Clare is an associate professor of English at the University of Washington, Seattle. She is a feminist, queer, and trans theorist and the author of *Earthly Encounters: Sensation, Feminist Theory, and the Anthropocene* (2019). Her current book project, *Non-Binary Wo/man: An Autotheory*, is forthcoming with Cambridge University Press.

Patrick R. Grzanka is a professor in the Department of Psychology at the University of Tennessee, where he is also chair of the Interdisciplinary Program in Women, Gender, and Sexuality. His current book project, *The "Born This Way" Wars: Sexuality, Science, and the Future of Equality* (under advance contract with Cambridge University Press), explores the affective and political investments that shape the pursuit of sexuality's biogenetic origins. Terminally undisciplined, he holds a PhD in American studies and BA in journalism, both from the University of Maryland.

Emmett Harsin Drager is a postdoctoral fellow of trans and queer studies in the Department of Women's and Gender Studies at the University of Missouri. Their work can be found in *Transgender Studies Quarterly* and the anthology *Turning Archival: The Life of the Historical in Queer Studies*.

Benjamin Kahan is Robert Penn Warren Professor of English and women's, gender, and sexuality studies at Louisiana State University. He is the author of *Celibacies: American Modernism and Sexual Life* (2013) and *The Book of Minor Perverts: Sexology, Etiology, and the Emergences of Sexuality* (2019). He is also the editor of *Heinrich Kaan's "Psychopathia Sexualis" (1844): A Classic Text in the History of Sexuality* (2016), *The Cambridge History of Queer American Literature* (under contract), and a coeditor of Theory Q, a book series from Duke University Press.

Greta LaFleur is associate professor of American studies at Yale University. LaFleur is the author of *The Natural History of Sexuality in Early America* (2018) and the coeditor of *Trans Historical: Gender Plurality Before the Modern*, *Nineteenth-Century American Literature in Transition, Vol. 1*, and prior special issues of *American Quarterly* and *Transgender Studies Quarterly*.

Rovel Sequeira is LSA Collegiate Postdoctoral Fellow and incoming assistant professor in the Department of Women's and Gender Studies at the University of Michigan, Ann Arbor. Rovel is currently working on a book manuscript titled "The Nation and Its Deviants: Global Sexology and the Racial Grammar of Sex in Colonial India," which foregrounds the intertwined circulation histories of sexual scientific and literary forms in producing nonliberal sexual and racial epistemologies in colonial and postcolonial South Asia. Rovel's work has appeared in *Modernism/modernity*; *Signs: Journal of Women in Culture and Society*; and *Museums, Sexuality, and Gender Activisms*.

Aaron J. Stone (they/them) is an affiliated scholar in the Lafayette College Department of English. They hold a PhD in English with a graduate certificate in LGBTQ studies from the University of Michigan. Their research spans queer and trans studies, multiethnic US literatures, modernist studies, and narrative theory. Stone's book project, "Desires for Form: Modernist Narrative and the Shape of Queer Life," examines the social crisis of form that Black and white queer subjects faced in early twentieth-century America and the narrative strategies these subjects employed in imagining what shapes their lives might take. Stone's work on drag performance is published in the collection *The Cultural Impact of RuPaul's Drag Race* (2021).

Jean-Thomas Tremblay is assistant professor of environmental humanities in York University's Department of Humanities. They are the author of *Breathing Aesthetics* (2022) and, along with Andrew Strombeck, a coeditor of *Avant-Gardes in Crisis: Art and Politics in the Long 1970s* (2021). They are currently working on two books: "The Art of Environmental Inaction" and, in collaboration with Steven Swarbrick, "Negative Life: The Cinema of Extinction."

Zohar Weiman-Kelman is a senior lecturer in the Department of Foreign Literatures and Linguistics at Ben-Gurion University of the Negev. They received a PhD in comparative literature from the University of California, Berkeley, and were a post-doctoral fellow at the Centre for Jewish Studies and the Women and Gender Studies Institute at the University of Toronto. Zohar was a fellow at the Katz Center for Advanced Judaic Studies and an associate scholar at the Humanities Forum on Sex, both at the University of Pennsylvania. Their first book, *Queer Expectations: A Genealogy of Jewish Women's Poetry*, was published in 2018.

Joanna Wuest is an assistant professor of politics at Mount Holyoke College. She is currently writing a book for the University of Chicago Press titled "Born This Way: Science, Citizenship, and Inequality in the American LGBTQ+ Movement." This research will also be featured in a volume accompanying a special exhibit, "Code of Life: Who We Are and Could Become," at the German Hygiene Museum in Dresden (the exhibit runs February–September 2023). Her other academic work has appeared in *Perspectives on Politics*, *Politics and Gender*, *Law and Social Inquiry*, *Polity*, and *nonsite*.

DOI 10.1215/10642684-10144533